Contents

Centrefold

Reviews

Endpapers

POEMS

I have a dusty disc which played
will cry and cry and will not be switched off.
—Peter Porter

Sean O'Brien
Fantasia on a Theme of James Wright

There are miners still
In the underground rivers
Of West Moor and Palmersville.

There are guttering cap-lamps bound up in the roots
Where the coal is beginning again.
They are sinking slowly further

In between the shiftless seams,
To black pools in the bed of the world.
In their long home the miners are labouring still –

Gargling dust, going down in good order,
Their black-braided banners aloft,
Into flooding and firedamp, there to inherit

Once more the tiny corridors of the immense estate
They line with prints of Hedley's *Coming Home*.
We hardly hear of them.

There are the faint reports of spent economies,
Explosions in the ocean floor,
The thud of iron doors sealed once for all

On prayers and lamentation,
On pragmatism and the long noyade
Of a class which dreamed itself

Immortalized by want if nothing else.
The singing of the dead inside the earth
Is like the friction of great stones, or like the rush

Of water into newly opened darkness. Oh my brothers,
The living will never persuade them
That matters are otherwise, history done.

Sarah Maguire
Damascene

Centuries of barefoot pilgrims have walked
this white marble to the stuff of glass –

billowing, doubled in *hijab*, I look down
into the heavens' absolute descent.

Swarming aloft from the rink of the Umayyad Mosque
a dark crowd of pigeons rips

open the golden fabric of dusk –
figures scaling the last slow heat of September,

a heat heavy with the end of a summer's summer –
its dust now settling onto cupolas and pantiles,

onto the balconied, octagonal minaret
where Jesus, one day, will alight to bring Judgement.

In the greenish, underwater gloom of the Prayer Hall
the head of John the Baptist waits behind bars.

                *

How strange I am to myself here –
out of bounds, unknown.

Lost in the night streets of Damascus
I am a figment of shadows

cast by yellowing lamps
down pleated corridors of overlapping homes;

their whitewashed flanks are still warm from the sun –
breathing, intricate, woven from wattle and thatch.

*

In a room walled with carpets,
a room warm with the smell of shorn wool

and the mineral tincture of dyes –
he laid me on a *kilim*, and I bled.

Psoriasis

If a red rose lies at the heart of me,
it cannot bloom.

Speechless, unknown –
but for this roseate

plague on my knuckles
and knees,

shedding its bastard pollen
in my sheets;

colourless,
the wrong pain.

John Burnside
from Responses to Augustine of Hippo
Ama et fac quod vis

for Piritta Maavuori

The God of St Paul, who is
no respecter of persons,

might just as easily have been
the self

      – that loves what it will
and watches us quicken and fade
with the passing of time

as calmly as we watch our shadows form
and lengthen, with each shift and slant of light.

      *

      Silencio es argumento llevado a cabo por otros metodos
      —Emesto Guevara

What we intend
and what we allow to happen
is anyone's guess.

All week my voice was failing – first husky, then strained,
till it guttered away to a whisper

and disappeared;
              guttered away

this morning, when the snow began to fall,
whiting out streets and gardens, muffling the cars,

until it seemed the only good reply
was silence:
        not

the quiet of dismay,
but what Guevara thought of as the argument
continued – *carried on*

by other means – that cold and salty pact
the body has with things unlike itself

– a snowfall, or a gust of Russian wind,
the evanescence of an upper room
that might be something new, or someone gone

a moment since
                    and how it is transformed
by what it never finds
                    – no soul; no
shadow:

                *

Propose what you like;
                    propose
causality
            the notion of the self
how one thing follows another
in grim succession

it only takes a moment in the wind
to break that argument.

Consider the body: changeable, incomplete,
yet still continuous:

think how it holds the perfect likenesses
of all the former selves that it is not,

how casually it gathers and renews
the forms we have scarcely noticed – winter buds,

a flock of starlings turning on the air,
the bleached grass skirting the lake
                            or the snake-bark of maples –

and how, on a morning like this, with our everyday lives
suspended
             in these white parentheses

we start again from scratch: the coming night;
the ferry that runs to the island;
                        the sullen ice;

the shapes we have scarcely noticed, bearing us on
to all we have yet to become
                        to the blank of a future.

                *

I wake in the dark and the dream evaporates before I can grasp the
                                                        details

– something about a bell, and prints in the snow;
my dream self distinct from the person I seem in waking;

my dream self, bright and light-footed,
a holy, unclouded soul, tracking these prints to the edge of a
                                        sycamore wood –

the details blurring and suddenly melting away
and only a moment's afterlife of joy:
the body a solid again, the mind a distraction,
the net of the slipshod entangling the peregrine heart.

                *

In the small hours,
awake and alone,

waiting for snow, or watching the snow as it falls,
from an upper room,

as far as I am from home,
and as strange as I seem,

what could I really prefer
to the weight of the self?

its deftness, on nights like this,
its immutable grace,

the only means I have
of bearing witness?

       *

This morning I followed a trail
to the edge of the woods,

then felt the shadow watching as I lost
my nerve:
           a brightness

slipped behind the rain;
an aftermath
          of lanolin and dust.

       *

Now I look back from the warmth
of a scentless house

with something foreign
cradled in my chest

and wonder that I took its weight
for safety, all those nights I passed untouched

and dreaming,
like a calf lulled in the dark

while something sweet
unfolds along the blade,

lifeblood
        or rapture
taken for a song.

Coral Bracho

Coral Bracho (b. 1951, Mexico City) has published five collections since 1977. In 1981 she was awarded the Aguascalientes House of Culture Prize. Her most recent book, Ese espacio, ese jardín (2003), won the Xavier Villaurrutia Prize. She has worked in the Institute of Philological Research at the National Autonomous University and helped to compile the Dictionary of Mexican Spanish.

Water of Jellyfish

Water of jellyfish,
milky, sinuous water,
water of slippery borders; glassy thickness — Deliquescence
amid delightful outlines. Water — sumptuous water
of involvement, of languidness,

in calm densities. Water,
silky water, like lead in opaqueness, in heaviness — Mercurial; suspended
water, dawdling water. The seaweed
of the sparkling — In the udders of pleasure. The seaweed, the breath of
its crest;

— over the arching silence, over the isthmuses
of basalt; the seaweed, the habit of its caress,
its gentle flux. Water of light, of fish; the breeze, the agate,
oozing light; The fleeting elk traces

fire — Amid the ceiba tree, amid the shoal; pulsing
flame;
lynx-like water, water of bream (Sudden jasper). Radiance
among the jellyfish.
—Open-lipped coastline; a breeze of slippery contours,
its rocking smoothness crystallizes as it settles; amphibious,
lubricious — Water, silky water
magnetized; alert. Suspended water, — Lascivious radiance

in the oily crossing
over capsizing basalt. — The opal crawls through the light,
through the internal flame. — Water
of jellyfish.
Soft, lustrous water;
water that leaves no trace; dense,
mercurial
   its steely whiteness, its diffusion in swellings of graphite,
in glimpses of minnows; furtive, smooth. — Live water

head over heels, bronze sun overturned embracing
— water of zinc, bursting. Water of jellyfish, tactile water
merging with itself
in unctuous indigo, shuddering honeycomb. Fibrous water, sea lettuce
The catfish bedded down
— sucking; in the nutritious fluid, in its delicate nectar; the golden
reservoir, a limbo, reveals it. Buoyant water, breeze inside the amber
— anointed luminosity, graceful; tiger, its high tide
beneath a glaze of shadow. Water of the frontier, eel water licking its
                                   own profile,
its nocturnal journey
— Amid the matrices of silk; amid the sea sage. — Water

amid hake. Gravid water (— Calm, warm
pleasure; irridescence) — Water
its borders

— Its mutating smoothness, charming itself
amid cadenced
ripeness. Water,
silky water, of involvement, of languidness,
in calm densities. Water, water; Its caress
— Water of otter, water of fish. Water

of jellyfish,
milky, sinuous water; Water,

Translated by Tom Boll and the Poetry Translation Centre Workshop

Yang Lian
Stroller

from Lee Valley Poems

Whether the golden fish sing about the rise and fall of the city or not
a line of swans on the riverbank study the book of their feathers
whether they model girls with mirrors or not
the stroller's self is filled completely by the sound of the wind
    led by a pitch-dark street
towards this stretch of marshland   where feet sink in an inch
the banks overflow with green which knows winter's weakness only too well
after the rain   the grassblades kneel on broken knees
one cloud invents an eclipse
the horizon watches him abruptly change between light and dark
    breeding a night
    in which a wild goose calls him continuously
towards this act of forgetting
feeling softly swallowed by the valley
feeling he has already become the valley   an empty willow
whose golden explosion throws out a womb endlessly giving birth to the sky
    listening to the wooden fence shout in the wind
    so nailed to death it stops the day
he arrives at the shared wetness of water and blood
where drowning waits   the chattering future a little bar
with a locked door   he is the entire city holding a stone cold cup
    as though planted, panting
walking further to be buried in the skeleton of an old iron bridge
walking impossibly further   rusty blood-red bushes
burst through his window   ghost-like sunlight appears once
revealing the swollen dark water-level settled over his head
    the drowned landscape is here
    in the dark the separated
        lonely hanging step is here

Translated by W. N. Herbert

Katherine Gallagher
Horizontal – (1924)

after Kandinsky

Chimneys, spires, half moons, lean over you
holding the idea of settlement together.

It is night and the city has put itself to bed
once more. Those who have survived

are in their shelters.
When you feel the dream slipping,

you are most endangered. Your enemies
and friends know it. If you lose your balance,

reach for the nearest horizontal.
Nothing, you tell yourself, can save you

from the war about to start.

Abdulah Sidran

Abdulah Sidran (b. 1944, Sarajevo) is an internationally renowned writer of screenplays as well as the senior living Bosnian poet. His major poetry collections are: Sahbaza, Bone and Meat, The Sarajevo Tomb *and* Why Venice is Sinking (Zašto tone Venecija). *His award-winning screenplays include* When Father was Away on Business *and* Do You Remember Dolly Bell? *directed by Emir Kusturica, and* Kuduz *and the* Perfect Circle, *directed by Ademir Kenovi.*

A Dispute About God

I
The other day some serious people remarked:
there's no God. Silence fell for thousands

and thousands of years, a briefer span
than a fragment fallen from a moment.

Then from silence, music's likeness, or its brother,
emerged and was the soul of sound itself.

Some sharp listener – no one special, that is how
he came to hear it – swore upon his mother's deafness,

with laughter shivering his face, he'd caught
within the silence, within the music, a whisper absolutely

human, except it sounded not
like something from a human throat – but God's.

II
So tell me, why would anyone wish God away?
I can think, dream, plan and manufacture

anything I like, but an absence that size,
in thoughts or reveries, I'd never have thought

to think of. Names confirm already
some kind of presence, don't they? God or Gods?

No particular skills are needed to count them.
Allow me this: two versions need to be considered –

One, as many Gods as people actually exist.
Two, which simplifies the matter somewhat,

there are just two: one who does exist and therefore gives,
and one who doesn't give and therefore can't exist.

These aren't just castles in the air, you know –
two versions, as I said, and neither starts from nowhere...!

III
Is this the measure of your thought:
God's been selling you – all these millenia –

short on the truth? He's visible, but actually
does not exist? He's not visible

but does? A deliberate absence? Or is he
just a brandy-drinking sot? That drunkard, dying

miserably on waste ground in between
those handsome churches? (Telling *them*

apart, I have to say, from the inside
or the outside, would be an utter waste

of time, you'd really need to want
to do it.) Your conclusion, anyway:

God's not here? No point, then, looking for his house,
his roof. (No chimney, no smoke.) Abandon it – this

enterprise. Or *see*. Observe the inconceivable.
He is – quite simply – there in everything – ungraspable.

IV

What follows threw me into something like confusion.
Needing something other than illusion, I reached

for certainty. Therefore: in the beginning was the Word.
Hills humped up, oceans swam round,

for ages flora hesitated, fauna even longer. Nobody
could hear it, but they say from everything a music

floated out. The player clearly knew just why he played
the tune he played. Music drove the world,

the world was driven by the music. Oceans got busy.
Birds flew. Beasts howled. (Plant power was proof

of something, too.) Let there be fish, beasts and birds –
and there they were! The skies spread everywhere,

and everywhere the Word (the Music, too) propelled the scene.
Only then – and only just in time, perhaps – man came by

and firmly grasped it. Tamed hills and water.
Carved out roads. Made countless languages

with a cautious tongue-tip. Made vessels that could
sail, then flew. Spoke the (sense-expanding) Word.

So don't defy *The One Who's Definitely There*. He moves.
In beasts, clouds, breasts and heaven: he is. The fact: He Does Exist.

V

Well, this isn't just a matter where you point.
Where you cry: *Look!* Some of it you have to offer

in the form of prayer. What's clear, now, is
that there was music, that it's lasted, that it

doesn't matter whether a player played it,
or whether it just played itself, that it still is

playing, that at least two gods exist: The One
Who Does and the one who doesn't. Useless to waste

time upon the latter, who neither cures nor causes
our *malheur*. He isn't here, but neither is he not here.

And not too many words about the former, either, except
he certainly exists, his apparition nothing like a man,

but like a word pronounced within the rich unfold-
ing of a voice. *"I exist. I am. Let your soul be pure."*

"Let your soul be pure. I exist. I am."
Through the medium of reverie he comes to me, taking

me apart as if I'd never been, and then re-
making me completely, the same bone, the same

meat in the same parcel of skin, assembled from the
same pain. Turning night to day, he makes me see

everything, my own death even, how and why
it will happen. For the hundredth time, I wake

at twenty to three in my ripped bed, soaked in sweat,
collecting my thoughts for the hundredth time: Sidran?

Is this you? Is this your bed? When all the ships
sink, when the world totters and falls, he is the one

who will stay close to your soul. Yes, he exists – how much
of him there is! – in a poet's fingers, scribbling

a song, everywhere, always, here and now, neither
substance nor a symbol, yet still the kindly and existing one

whose artful care enables me to bear the pain of being,
who leads me, lamb-like, to the end of being.

Translated by John Hartley Williams

Pascale Petit
War Horse

after Franz Marc

Yesterday, I saw a horse die –
the most fiery but obedient white Pegasus

groaned in great pain like a human
wakened from a vivid dream.

Now he is a stinking corpse.
Nights, I sleep in the meadow.

When it's quiet, the stars open.
They are my flowers. Darling –

when you look at our garden,
think of me looking up at mine.

Have you seen the War-Comet?
Bigger than Halley's,

it follows us over the fields of France.
It has an icy mane.

Conversation:
Cars, Trains and maybe Planes

Elizabeth Smither
Horse Playing the Accordion

That's something you don't often see
as the courtesy car goes past
the low steps of the Festival Hall:
a horse playing the accordion.

A beautiful black horse's head
so elegant and refined: its profile
would break your heart if he turned
or lifted his hands from the accordion

which is red and yellow, quite dainty,
and his tunic – like a medieval page –
a dried blood red – his stockings
below his knee breeches, white and red

Saturn rings – everything is pathos
everything so designed to bring together
the horse playing the accordion
with a hat – black, wide-brimmed –

for donations, casually at his
feet or hooves. Let me out.
I want to give everything in my purse
to the beautiful horse and his accordion.

Colette Bryce
Car Wash

This business of driving
reminds us of our fathers.
The low purr of fifth gear,
the sharp fumes, the biscuity
interior, has brought them,
ever-absent, nearer.
And has brought us, two women
in our thirties, to this
strange pass, a car wash
in Belfast; where we've puzzled
and opted for "Executive
Service" (meaning
detergent) and have minded
the instructions to wind up
our windows and sit
tight when the red light
shows, and find ourselves
delighted by a wholly
unexpected privacy
of soap suds pouring, no,
cascading in velvety waves.

And when spinning blue brushes
of gargantuan dimensions
are approaching the vehicle
from all directions,
what can we do
but engage in a kiss
in a world where to do so
is still seen as shocking;
then into the rinse,
and in view once again
of the idling motorists
queuing on the forecourt,
we are polished and finished

and (following instructions)
start the ignition (which
reminds us of our fathers)
and get into gear
and we're off
                    at the green light –

Kapka Kassabova
Love in the Dark Country

Tomorrow for twenty-four hours
I'll be in the same country as you,

The sky will be constantly shifting,
the morning will be green, a single morning
for my single bed. And in the night

as the dark country goes to sleep
a church bell will measure
the jet-lag of my heart.

I'll open my suitcase and unfold my life
like a blanket. In the dark country I will lie
all night and wonder how this came to be:

the one light left in the world
is your window, somewhere in the land

of thin rain and expensive trains,
and instead of maps, I have an onward ticket.

Menna Elfyn
Journey by Car

An old journey, with an old man.

We journey through the country,
setting the sure clock
to check the ground we cover.

And no matter how numerous the miles,
they unspool beside the years
of this elder in whose eyes all buildings

are dilapidated, mere ruins –
'closed' is his word for the day,
seeing chapel and church and meeting house

backslide into carpet shop
or the dentistry that, tooth in cheek,
gives him a text for a sermon

sealed under the roof of his mouth:
how the sainted ones should brush their teeth
lest they claim a tooth for a tooth.

Is this how it is for the meek ones
who cross that ninety-year road?
Each closure a shaky foot on a rung,

stepping backwards, backwards, back, back
to the old body of the past.
'What shall I do with all these memories?'

he sighs, knowing full well
that he can't contain them as names fade, dates collide.
And yet there's plenty to share out,

'Too many memories is what I have.
Every day, I try and say under my breath,
"No going back today, now,

Just steer along, steer along, embrace the day."'
And I know too how the mercury of the hour
is difficult as decimal to handle.

Ninety years down the road, here he is,
his century of splendour spent,
orchard idle now, bruised apples uncollected.

                    *

Look on, I say to myself, we'll be there one day,
belted in, too old to worry
at the dizzying speed of the hedges.

Will we see the Millennium Centre shine
like a crown under water, reflective baldness?
Will the National Library close

from a lack of interest in pages:
or will it, one night, burst into flames?
And who knows, will we echo 'closed', 'closed'

to this and that as the scattered ruins
lie over the little greenery there is,
as hard and grey as lichen?

Throughout our lives, we live in reverse
on the eternal way, the golden mile
that suddenly becomes a single track road,

and find ourselves backing
to a passing place to wait, rather than block the lane.
Metre by metre, we find our way home

knowing that, for us here on earth, everything
comes and goes, the opening, the closing;
and at that we too open the car door

then shut it quickly – feebly at first,
the second time giving it a good bang –
just to be sure, just to be on the safe side

Translated by Elin ap Hywel

Eugenio Montale
The Bard

He's booked a first class berth
on the train which goes but doesn't return
from the great beyond.

He takes no luggage.
Only a pamphlet, of *morceaux choisis*,
with the authoritative blurbs

of *** and *** and *** and ***.
Up there, perhaps,
he will make a great impression.

Translated by Simon Carnell and Erica Segre

Valeria Melchioretto
Finding Myself in a Pair of Fisheyes

I arrive on the desperate island in the late afternoon.
Shadows are so long they have a sense of gravity.

The guidebook advises a visit to the twenty-two churches
built next to each other for comfort and I read

that the altars were carved from bone of unknown origin.
The last ferry to the mainland has already departed.

The waiter serves me a dozen grilled sardines. The recipe:
divorced from water and remarried by fire. I bless them

with lemon and seek out their skeletons. I throw salt
over my shoulder and wander to the only guesthouse in town.

I agree a price with the landlady. Her French sounds fake.
She shows me upstairs and taking a step at a time.

The room is clean and basic. I'm spellbound by the still
lives that adorn the square, furnished corridor. Five identical

flower paintings in hospital green and blood red on a clashing
background. I stay up all night, comparing them

maybe to find the answer to all questions concerning
individuality. I tiptoe, rub my eyes as if not to disturb

what lies behind those dying tulips: tulips as vivid
and wide awake as church-bells on a Sunday morning.

Ulrike Draesner

DANIE BISKUP

Ulrike Draesner (b. 1962, Munich) lives and works in Berlin. This poem is taken from her fourth collection of poetry, kugelblitz (ball lightning) (2005). She has published two volumes of short stories and two novels; a third, Spiele (Games) was published this year.

hyacinth colic

you slept still i sat
your breath was going day
was pushing forest fieldward
the meadow now began
to flash in shadow fed a
pair of pigeons she with claws
so hot a small fleck on his
neck. still soft their calls
as dear as childhood mornings
(all asleep but sun and
dove and quiet roof) you
went your chest was oiled
nude you went the disc had
struck his forehead cooled
and warmed and hardened.
trying is a game the guilt and
every bed on floors is hard in
its pot the hyacinth is testing
whether quite without you
i will bear its scent

Translated by Iain Galbraith

Tim Liardet
Ground Bass

Having confessed to the killing of some fifty five people, though adjudged
legally sane, created – it has been said – by the excesses of Soviet famine
and deprivation, Chikatilo was taken to the Serbsky Institute in Moscow
for psychiatric evaluation…
        —*New York Times,* October 1992

Don't talk to me of the soul; that after all
is the business of saints. Do you imagine it squats
on the shelf, thick with the beautiful references?

I think it moves the left half of the brain which moves
the right, etcetera. Through your two-way glass,
gentlemen, I was the wrong way around,

and though the left half of the brain is held responsible
for the actions of the right half of the body
I was confused as to what was left,

what right, what normally sloped one way
sloping the other. That mouth. Oh, I note your eyes
slip away in one movement and look down

as you throw a leg across the other, and sigh,
and brush your sleeves… windblown
and still recovering from the eleven flights

which lead you down, not up, and place
such a strain upon the muscles of the calf…
better, though, perhaps than that

secateurs of a lift (I see you smile)
which brings you down, down through the centre
of this old building by the light

of a flickering forty watt bulb which still
somehow refuses to blow.
                              I cause, I know,
your keyboards to click more avidly of late,

tracking white with bright ideas or shunting
the carriages which jostle and bump
and stall behind the cursor's engine

towards the slow ascent and descent
of understanding. I am the stump in mist
even your rainswell cannot dislodge

when everything floods like the yellow Grushevska
roaring at such a speed it swept away
and then washed up the evidence;

what I had sent out was brought back,
brought back, and ducked me towards
the final enfilade of flash-cubes in the snow:

Chikatilo the frozen. Prize of the Public
Prosecutor's Office. They say I have two souls.
One plausible tenth, they say, Andrei Romanovich

shows us by the light of day
while the other nine are out of sight...
You must forgive me. Your appetite of course

is one that has no bottom at all,
as if with each fresh morsel, full of protein,
the stone in the belly is appeased

but never fully satisfied, being stonelike.
Little Lena Zakotnova, Larisa Tkachenko,
bewildered Lyuba Biryuk in her thirteenth year,

Ivan Beletski picking apricots in sunlight
and the other fifty-one who strolled too close
to the centre, who rolled over one by one

in their skeins of drenched hair,
cling to my belt-buckle, cuffs, my fingertips
The mortician's label is attached to their toes.

Should I continue? I think there is
something of the prurient priest at large
in your questioning, offended by what

most attracts and is enough to drop
your young assistant's elbow on the zero-key
of the machine which trundled in his lap

but now sends out (though he doesn't know it)
a flat line of zeros across the screen
beyond the last recorded intelligence

while he sips at his mug with startled eyes:
how is he to know, when the succession of noughts
suddenly jumps onto its second line

and then a third and then a fourth and fifth,
language has failed, and a new sort of wilderness
is being created as it is discovered

a centimetre at a time, offering no
distinguishing features or signs of life,
just more, just more and more of the same?

I give you what you most seem to want;
I give you what I give you.
                          The lift goes down.
I grew, that is to say, I grew there

in growth-spurts of infinite slowness
far from the dangerous surface:
beneath the upper light my glacial will

was legumes of stretched rock, so long
and tapering, like organ pipes sipping frozen water,
and the mile of my small intestine

wound down, down, in rock-folds
smooth as marble or polished obsidian
towards the crystal cave of the duodenum

thick with a white profusion
of snow-flowers along to the holly-like nibs of which
a gathering plump drip rolled

its undiluted acid – and froze:
the unusually developed (...it is said)
cerebellum bloomed in an overhead drapery

of frozen folia, shedding a fine frost...
Your lamps shine into me. I am
the spectacular efflorescence

of your spirits' boredom. Note how
your voices drop in my company
like Sunday hats removed in reverence, how

the fishmonger treasures my till receipt
and others my clippings, a single hair, a relic,
any faintest, obscurest relic of me

while the crowds trail past my door
as if my rarity were the wonder
and a certain sort of status conferred

by touching it, even by drawing close.
You greet me, shall we say, somewhere between
cunosity and fear – disturbed and intrigued

by a man with knowledge of the depths.
I grew too slowly,
                         while everything sped.
When the world developed requirements

it could neither articulate nor meet
I knew I had grown out of want
and I knew I had grown slowly enough

to do the dirty work, to wring the surplus
of moisture from Christ's sponge
though your hands, shall we say, were clean... it must

be fine to sit in your self-angelising
seat, clean-cuffed and manicured, confident your hands
will never be grubbied, shuffling papers...

When I lift my left foot in its chains
a tram stalls in rainy Rostov, then starts again.
Shortly, gentlemen, you'll squeal your chair-legs

and depart, gathering up your effects
and rewinding your machine, leaving me
to the very last of my several attempts

to prolong the conversation... words dissolving
with my latest expression, fade by fade,
though held in your magnetic signal

like the voice from the other side, to be
played over and over for the clue.
Tape me a moment longer, though your eyes betray

involvement inflected with unease,
a weariness laced with tact...
What of the age, I ask you, which demands a beast

more slyly itself, more extravagant,
to manage needs so complex?
I felt my acts drawn larger, as if a pantograph

first set down the point that followed
every crevice and outline of each act
while the second point, as if instructed,

enlarged it perhaps some twenty times:
and the arms that linked the two pistoned back
and plunged like mechanical elbows

on their swivelling rivets; so both continued
moving as one, faithful to every detail
the first discovered at the tip of its point

and the second merely reproduced,
until the gadget completed the outline both
of the act and its intricate implications

the more you looked, as if you looked through
the atoms at exploded atoms beneath
and saw some terrible truth there.

Sometimes I dreamt it was God.
Or perhaps a minor, unassuming god
sometimes inclined to whisper a little

of the flame that could burn a halo
out of these zero temperatures
– now orange, now yellow, now blue –

or flare up, of a sudden, like caught gas
and burn away my stained cape,
and burn away my hands, and burn away my feet,

and burn away my body out of which
a body might grow, warmed on one side
to a sort of rosy flush by the flame

that infuses crystal with creeping colour
and bursts from the frozen heart itself
and fills my mouth.

Peter Porter
Discs with Everything

Moses had a trusted follower
at a level lower than his own
who helped to carry down the Decalogue
from Sinai. What's not well-known
is that the Tablets this time came
with special offers, if he filled the form in,
of incisive and assured declensions
of parallel religions from established
and adjacent states, Assyria, Egypt
and a place called Pontus. He shook them out
over his waste-papyrus basket –
they made quite a clatter. Nothing, he said,
can match the matchless offers of the Lord.

Later there were so many unsolicited
additionals to be discounted.
Along with his *Vita Nuova*, Dante
was obliged to include a CD
of extracts from the *Summa Theologica*
and an offer of a year's subscription
to the whole concordance. *Paradise Lost*
was similarly intruded on
by *Affairs of State* in tiny type
endorsed by Andrew Marvell
on reproduction House-of-Commons-
headed paper. Many decades on, *Mein Kampf*
was outweighed by its onanist inclusions.

Today we know that when tomorrow dawns
all separate offers will be off –
a crowded planet's just an insight
into Heaven or its still invisible
other side, as Hell, and souls will be
unseparate as Blake's hunched grains of sand.
But this we cannot feel because we clutch
our own *Complete and Finished Works*
and have been promised readership
and plaudits. Is it my impulsive notes,
my sugared sonnets or my wizened words
you'll love? I have a dusty disc which played
will cry and cry and will not be switched off.

Ellen Hinsey
A Short Primary on Imagination and Destruction

1.
Prima Facie

Not every act, performed in hostage to the mind, can be contained in language.

2.
Lexicography

That which exists on the periphery of language is a shade; forced to wander eternally in a terror of disclosure.

3.
Transmission

What remains unspoken in consciousness passes, like a form of inheritance, into the estate of common being.

4.
Perplexing Paradox

That which eludes language exerts an impossible weight on the centre of speech.

5.
Cause and Effect

Heraclitus believed that, in the end, all matter would be burned in the crux of time.

6.
Fallible Corollary

That which resists being revealed must one day be burned up in utterance.

7.
Paradox of Grief
To speak is an impossible form of renewal. *What has been done cannot be restored by language.*

To speak is essential to affirm the *potential of utterance*, which is its own capital.

8.
Report
In obscure night he fell, his entrails spilled, his blood filling the furrows of earth dark red.

9.
Regnum Imaginarii
Imagination is subject to its own sovereign laws: not all that is executed can be *imagined.*

10.
Event
Clawing the dust, life flew from him—and the weight of hateful darkness closed in.

11.
Petrification
The imagination, stunned, drew its shield up against the writhings of the mind.

12.
Nunc et Semper
Do not speak of it – it was unimaginable.

John Fuller
Brahms in Thun

Who is that singular man upon the path
Winding from Hofstetten, his long black coat
Greying with age, the shawl over his shoulders
Fastened with a pin? The flannel shirt
Collarless, and the shabby leather satchel
Surely full of bohemian mysteries?

The urchins know who he is. He shoos them away
With the hat that's always in his pudgy hand.
The girls know who he is. When he draws near,
A trifle corpulent, full-bearded, grey,
They notice with a flutter of the heart
The piercing blue eyes of a younger man.

Who certainly notices them. He gives a bow,
A brief acknowledgment of what their eyes
Have searched for in his eyes. Then looks away.
This is not the time, nor ever will be,
For words to rob the unspoken melody
Of its elusive and absorbing fragrance.

It haunts him now. Its cadences arrive
Like the brief mysteries of flowers in spring,
Frail for the buttonhole, their scent soon gone.
But now in the dust of summer let him stand
And let the petals open, let them fall
In all their fullness to the reaching hand.

This morning, stepping from the deep-eaved villa
Rented from Herr Spring, half in its shadow,
He paused just for a moment, lit a cigar
And breathed at once the air and its aroma.
This is the mood of amiable resolution,
The piano as portico to an adventure.

He feels that he might stroke the Wellingtonia,
Whose roots beneath the hill drink in the lake,
While here by the railings at megalosaurus's height
Its branches stir in their Jurassic calm;
Stroke its rough hide as if it gave off sound,
As if the pine were strung to its very tip.

Even now the smoke continues its
Vague dispersal through the shadowed tree,
Lofting minutest particles in the warm air
To the pine's pinnacle, where the needles cease.
Although now he has passed along the path,
The stride determined, tobacco in clouds about him.

The tiles of the Thunerhof below are severe
To the meditative eye, the circular divan
In the Bellevue salon equally distracting.
There the Knechtenhofers' assembled guests
Would eat the famous composer half-alive
To occupy the lateness of the morning.

"Milord Ponsonby would wish that he
Were here, as we ourselves are glad to be:
The great artist in sounds, the sheet of the lake
Covered with quavers of sails, a glass or two
To toast Vienna and to hear a tale
Of Elgin, ruins, and a grand concerto..."

A lion, then, among the jackals who
Would lift their jaws from working, prick their ears
At rumours of a richer feast elsewhere
And leave their crumbs of carrion behind
For the bored waiters of the Speiseterrasse.
Take heart: the Bains de Bellevue are not for him.

On, on, to the Schüssel in the Plätzli,
The beer ingratiating, dizzy and blond,
The company reliable, with shouting laughter,
The schnitzels overlapping their plates all round,
Heavy as dewlaps of long-slumbering hounds,
The flower fading on the creased lapel.

But in the mind, where flowers never fade,
There lives one favoured face that is a smile,
A smile that is a voice: "*O komme bald!*"
"Come soon, come soon! Before the May winds blow.
Before the thrush sings in the wood, oh come!
If you would see me once again, oh come!"

The voice is hers, and yet the song is his.
Who can be certain where the yearning lies?
Her lips are parted, and his notes come out.
Her throat swells with the thrilling melody
That will make others weep; so she and he
Survive their shout of grief, inviolable.

But is it grief? Not joy, perhaps? She gave
Him joy. He gave it back as if it were
Some sort of tender, self-inflicted wound:
"Often in my dreams I hear you calling,
Calling outside my door. But no-one wakes,
Nobody is awake to let you in."

What does he think they mean, these words?
Fate is in them, also resolution.
Death, too, is there, and also a wild hope:
"Come, then, for one last time, for you will find me
Gone from a world that has no place for us.
But if you come, oh if you come, come soon."

And will one come again, will such a one?
His Fraülein Spies, the charming Rhinemaiden,
Herma, Herminche, Hermione-ohne-o?
He follows her to Wiesbaden, full-tilt
At his Third Symphony, sets Groth for her.
He's never in his life written so fast.

And he'll produce her for the Widmanns (guilty
Of curiosity about the work
She has inspired). Rigorous torture by song's
Their punishment: the jovial composer
And his Krefeld songstress will come to them with skewers
("*Spiessen und stangen!*") next Wednesday after dinner.

Wonderful Thun… The steamer on the lake
Hoots at the afternoon; its paddles ply
The Aare to the harbour where he sees
Such parasols in clusters, greeting, retreating.
Beyond, a train is puffing into the station
Like an old gentleman expecting treats.

Later he might allow himself to walk
Down there again, a brandy at the Freienhof,
And in the Markt the smell of girls and herring.
And will one come again, will such a one?
It haunts him like something about to disappear.
He tries to put a name to it, but fails.

Perhaps it is something he has always missed,
The sound of laughter in another room,
Hands at his knee, hands tugging him away,
The playing, the watching, the kissing and the dancing,
The faces echoing their other faces,
That strange projection of the self, like art.

Some melodies are statements like the mountains,
The Stockhorn, Niesen, and the Blümlisalp,
Claiming their definition of the sky,
Others elusive as the mist which rises
Like half-remembered dreams from the still lake
In which the sky and mountains have been drowned.

And they exchange their notes in playful ways
That echo all these harmonies of nature
Where one thing, though itself, reveals another:
Fields broken by trees, forest by pasture,
The levels of the Aare linked by weirs,
Its course shaped both by broken land and water.

The little town itself, with its red roofs,
Rises like a flowering of the earth,
A human watchfulness that celebrates
The parting of the river from the lake
In boyish determination, that sees its future
Clear, and makes its watery business there.

And the Schloss, its profile out of fairy-tales,
Throws up its pointed turrets at the sky,
Casements of trance, imprisonment or longing
Where distance is for once the only meaning,
Its central slab of tiles uncannily
Matching the Stockhorn like a falling cadence.

And will one come again, will such a one?
And what on earth would happen if she did?
Herma, Herminche, Hermione-ohne-o,
The voice embodying the melody,
The melody abstracting from the heart,
The heart enchanted by an opening mouth.

"I am a man who's getting to those years
Where he quite easily does something stupid,
And so I have to doubly watch myself."
And Clara thinks she's being left in the cold,
Dear Clara, arbiter, his earliest muse,
Old lady at the keyboard in a cap.

Who, when her darling Robert in his slippers
Left her and ran out through the carnival
To throw his person into the Rhine and madness,
Preserved herself for music and her children,
Year upon year preparing for her concerts
Like a devoted priestess at the altar.

Who taught him out of tragedy to know
That feelings are firmly locked within the stave
Lest they uncover foulness: what would she say?
The fingers scramble like waves upon the shore,
Tides of regret advance to their conclusion,
Storming their beaches, where her profile bows.

There are mistakes too terrible to be made,
When to approach them, as to an upstairs room
Where light invites the idle passer-by,
Is to stand upon a brink of fascination
Whose logic is a desecration and
Whose music is a series of farewells.

All that this art in its bodily abstraction
Has seriously learned to do: to exult in pain
And be stoical in pleasure, to be triumphant
With propriety and reserved in ceremony,
To take grief into fury and out of it again,
He had for long with mastery acquired.

His mood now is a matter of resolution,
Where resolution has no certain hope
To pronounce an equal love impossible
In waves of thunder shot with trickles of light,
To embrace the damage of the soul with joy
And to erect the architecture of tenderness.

His hand moves over the page like a flock of birds
Seeking rest in snow, their tracks a relic
Of the enduring passage of a hunger
Across an infinite waste, a fragile heartbeat,
The Stockhorn, Niesen, and the Blümlisalp,
At once forbidding and familiar.

Quick, catch their flight... The hand continues to move,
The quavers swarm, the sheets fall from the piano,
The rhythms fight it out, the prey's in sight,
Crisp noble chords, the strings making decisions
That their invisible fingers lead them to,
The next idea that lies in wait for them.

The only respite is a dark *kaffee*.
The ritual itself is stimulating:
His brass pot from Vienna with its spigot;
Its porcelain stand; the little burner moving
Its blue flame like a crocus underneath;
The grinding of the mokka from Marseilles.

And a cigar, of course. And in its wreaths,
The music for a moment laid to rest,
He lives within the mood it has created:
And will one come again, will such a one?
And what on earth would happen if she did?
How to accommodate that bodied voice?

Herma, Herminche, Hermione-ohne-o!
Is it too late? Isn't the paradox
Just this: the one mistake committed is
The one that will transcend both fear and error
And in its act be no mistake at all?
And will one come again, will such a one?

Somewhere in his mind the names proceed
Like cases that have come to shape a law:
Clara, of course, Agathe, Julie, Lisl,
And all the singers of his Frauenchör
Whose voice and beauty caught his ear and eye,
Music's muses, music's priestesses.

They ring him round with their accusing looks.
He kneels before them in contrition, asking
Of song if the perfection of its moods
And of its utterance has power to
Redeem the soul of a defective man.
And song, as usual, has no sort of answer.

Nor does *kaffee*. And nor do Frau Widmann's buttery
Plum pastries. Nor does the Wellingtonia.
Nor does that broad and energising vista
Across the lake where paddle-steamers ply,
The Stockhorn, Niesen, and the Blümlisalp,
Each reassuring as a reputation.

For there it is. The music must be written.
And Fraülein Spies will have her début in
Vienna. And Karlsgasse Num. 4 is only
An old bear's den, almost a hermit's cell.
And the Bernese summer, like every summer since
The beginning of the world, will soon be over.

And with the summer over, who can say
What may be found in the satchel of mysteries?
Wonderful Thun... The watchful fairy Schloss,
The midwife of his own late blossoming,
Herma, Herminche, Hermione-ohne-o,
The Trio, the Sonatas, and the Songs.

"Come, then, for one last time, for you will find me
Gone from a world that has no place for us.
But if you come, oh if you come, come soon!"
The instruments inscribe their own enticements
Upon the holy movement of a heart
Too long alone to know when it is teasing.

"It comes to me, this thing, whatever it is,
Like the spring flowers that steal upon the senses
And drift like scent away. Then comes the word
That holds it before my eye until it pales
Like the grey mist, and like a scent it dies.
Yet still a tear calls fragrance from its bud."

That tear is music, emotion's memory,
And God forbid there should be story in it.
The good Herr Doktor with the forget-me-not eyes
Strides on, the emperor of a world of sound
So pure he scarcely sees that its grand truth
Is fatally wedded to the human voice.

Lawrence Sail
Sensed

1
At the turn of the path
where the earth becomes dusty...

Where is the thinking ghost,
the shadow self?

Each chime of the clock
a dent hammered into
the smooth surface of dreaming

And the thick fragrance
of night-flowers flooding the garden...

Who is lying, heart racing,
in the room with drawn curtains?

At the turn of the path
where the trees close in
all your possible dreams are hidden

2
The wind falters in the leaves
a voice trailing
into forgetfulness

Hanks of rain drive
over the dark
lure of the lake

Hardly to be glimpsed, a hand
draws heavy
curtains closer

In the leaves, the wind begins
to stir again, squaring
up to the night

Robert Minhinnick
The Dolphin

It's not the shadow of a cloud or the shape of a shoal
so I ask what's out there –
as if the answer was concealed within myself.

I ask myself what it might be
and after a while it is the swimmer that replies,
daring to show its deft muscle and delphic arc.

Next I start counting with my own heartbeat
and discover that every ten seconds this swimmer surfaces
like a bowsaw against the sea's green grain,
and that every ten seconds it leaps eastward
off the rocks of Cyrn y locs towards The Irongate.

There are fathoms between us
but we are familiars. I am sure of that.
Because I have walked where it dives now
and I have swam where it is swimming
through the grey wall slow to fall in rubble,
through the white wall it has mined yet flies above.

And every ten seconds this dark dauphin
of the gwters and the gwlis and the grykes,
every ten seconds the Gulf Stream leopard
hurtles out of the salt thickets
and from where I stand on the cliff's dais
I can feel it coming, I can feel it coming,
so that the sea is changed and will never be the same.

Because here is the oracle of an ordinary tide –
something that cuts a crescent like the dark of the moon.
Then exultant in the air we both must breathe
is the polished ferrule of the dolphin's face.

John Kinsella
Ugliness – A Vision

The terror of road-widening
to lessen the death toll, tricks
of the developer popping up like the exquisite
feel of losing control as you round the corner:
a high-risk accidental manoeuvre you feel
like doing again,
                      as if merycism is not a disorder
but a joy – a chewing the cud of beauty,
the way something goes in and is forced out
with explosive sensation –
          going from loose gravel
to sand after torrential rain,
              sown fields weltering
and saying we'll crisp harder
                 when drought reconstitutes,
ninety degrees at the crossroads
bowing out to one hundred
then one hundred and five
and the back end
pushing
        the heart into the mouth,
processing the angles
   and circumferences of correction,
             knowing what's left in the keel-hauling
of "land" is the celebration
purely on the level
of the single cell,
        behest of protoplasm,
            an argument or irritation
shifting response that deadly degree,
        the arc of a kite exquisite,
frankly beautiful;
so, what's made of a bricolage
        of death, sex, compound fractures
of vision and selfishness?

Of the ascetic's prayer-
incantation
when sleep comes down, shut-eyed
screen of collision,
the unseemly tree warped by high winds,
fire, the brutality of axes and children – maybe *you*
thirty or so years earlier –
bush-bashing
the road's edge like a cult, crossroads
its vaticinal emblem –
in *that* corner of bush we trapped…
and checked the traps cold at daylight,
macarised blood on teeth as ugly as…
and souveniring a rabbit's foot
to empower in a split second
city-school emasculations,
so smooth if stroked
the right way, though pressed hard
the bone disturbing the insides
of touch, prospects of luck;
widening
the road, they celebrate safety,
tap down less deeply,
level rabbit warrens
with split levels, rectitude, consistency.

Deluge (Cant)

Instantaneous and not seeing.
                              A torrent
in the aqueous humour. A shindig of light
and graven images.
            What gaze owned by fixation
                    on gauze covering,
through a black veil the white moons shifting
as caught out, makes apprehension?
                              Though purple-black,
                    clouds violent above the house on the crest
        of the hill: bloating, restive in its cradle.
Drenched, there are no nerve endings
            to carry sound,
                    to elongate
            dramatic weather conditions,
the nation's "top scientist", slipping
back into the mining industry
            from whence he came;
                                    impact
                    mushrooms
                and enwraps, no needlepoint,
            whiling
away of evenings, candlelight
barely enough, to burn through
and coat the skin warm with friction,
suddenly cold when floodwaters
puddle
            around your feet;
                    drought keeps hocking
its old goods in the narrowing catchment,
                        drought is sodden fleece
trailing out ribcage, resolved internal organs: the wick
            tapping barometer, nostalgia
                    of fellow sheep – living – bracketed
around a powderbark, edge of gathered materials –
the reserve – agitate appendix and appendices,

                    bodily opening out,
                            worth capturing
a moment the mind clears, thinking
                    dynamic: downpour has stopped,
                            hemi-commandment
            has us cowering
                            beneath white-tailed cockatoos
            further
north-east than we'd imagine (pro bono storms
that mantle, and still to come), no fear,
no quota,
                    no restorative qualities of faith
gone up with the deluge,
                            going under?

Sheenagh Pugh
Interviewing The Two Last Speakers

The young researcher, in at the death,
can't credit his luck. A language,

a whole language, passing out of use,
out of knowledge, unless he can catch

each mumbled word of these old women
as it falls, and fix it in print,

where it will forget how to elude
definition, change colour, grow

new subtleties. He's sad for the words,
pinned down on paper, but he thrills

to hear them spoken. His fingers
cramp, trying to keep up: *goodbye*

is gendered; come rhymes with go
and nothing declines in the plural.

Two columns in his notebook: two
old women giving him words,

the two last speakers. Often
they differ; an accent will shift

the word's shape, a memory
turn a meaning. In his riches

he longs for more: a conversation,
words picked up, sent back, two voices

fusing or sparking. It can't be,
he knows: the two last speakers,

loathing each other, have not met
or talked in years. This speech will never

again be current, a conduit
for thought, anger, wit. He takes notes

while there's still time: *the verb
to lose has no present tense.*

Paul Henry
Morfudd, 2005

Allow me to translate myself,
the wind through bare branches.
I knock about this tiny house
with a mirror held up to my face.
I was blessed with two tongues,
a *cariad* in the north
and a lover in the south.
Both wear red waistcoats
that drip like blood about them
in the breeze of twin farmyards.
And both cut me in half
when we make love. Is it they
or I who got displaced?
I leave them to their different songs,
their beds, their half-dug trenches –
one spade travelling north
the other south – half-thrilled
and half filled with dread
at this vision I have
of them knocking through soil
to meet, like escapees
completing the same tunnel.

cariad – lover (Welsh)

Martha Kapos
Lost in South Devon

When I'm facing you
In bed, you slip out through
The trajectory of your eye –
Its path shoots off on a journey
Of its own around the room,
Settles for a moment lightly
On the floor, describes
A curve and, talking freely now
In conversation with the air,
Floats long spiral stories
Through the window; they escape
Like smoke. Spooling out
Your eye unwinds your body
Like a ball of string.
It goes about fast and far-flung.
It cruises the possibilities like a dog
Let out first thing into the park;
Thought catching sight of thought
And pulling, it locks the mind
Into being what it sees.
Now the world is entering your face.
You stare back through
The open door as hard as daylight.
Shining black from last night's rain
Your eye walks out abundantly in leaf
Along a branch, dwindles
To a narrow stem then disappears
Into any tight slit of sky
The green shade lets you through.
Out there you've never been
So pure as this
Blank blue racing overhead,

So sharp and pencil-thin
As this horizon. The shoreline
Of your body now comes, goes, climbs
Steep air and curls itself
Around clouds. There's no stopping you
Lighting on the sea and leaping
Dark and blue. Soon you'll be smashing
Your head. Down on your knees
You'll be rolling in to the beach
Bubbles popping your skin
Like the definition of joy.
I want you back – walled
Inside your heart, tucked securely
Under the covers of your skin.
Keep still inside
Your given name, not this insane
Unravelling.

Joanne Limburg
Milk

The nurse taps my foot
every two hours.
Time to draw out
a little of me.

Every two hours,
20 by cup,
a little of me,
a note on a chart.

20 by cup.
His mother is
a note on a chart,
a dream of a face.

His mother is
not yet all there:
a dream of a face
floats behind glass.

Not yet all there,
the hospital's baby
floats behind glass,
swaddled in heat.

The hospital's baby
has to remain
swaddled in heat.
This cannula

has to remain
on his tiny arm,
this cannula,
an outsized claw.

On his tiny arm,
my own hand seems
an outsized claw,
too crude a tool.

My own hand seems
no good at all.
Too crude a tool,
the hand pump creaks.

No good at all:
the barest trickle.
The hand pump creaks.
It's nearly one.

The barest trickle
for my own flesh.
It's nearly one.
They send me to bed.

For my own flesh,
never enough.
They send me to bed.
I drift into sleep.

Never enough
time to draw out.
I drift into sleep.
The nurse taps my foot.

R. D. Coleman
Going North

i
going north on the west side drive
just before eight thirty a,m.
the police have stopped all south bound traffic
cold. highway patrolmen in leather boots
stand on the roadway. the back-up... I think...
there was an accident, I thought.

ii
memory kicks up visions that never have happened,
parades them as real before us; pushes real events
somewhere inside and may never free them again.
I remember not understanding why the cars were held.
southbound, not northbound. I don't remember
the radio on. I always turn it on in the car.
I made the turn to the cross bronx, and then
to the deegan and continued on to my mechanic's.

iii
Jarida says he hasn't come in yet,
that a plane had hit one of the world trade towers.
it was still sounding like an accident; a b-24 once hit
the empire state. of course, it had to be an accident.
the shop is under the el on jerome. and I normally
leave the car, catch a train, change once, and wind up
my own corner. bronx to manhattan, thirty five
to forty minutes.

iv
as I left the shop, a tram rumbles by, and by
the time I'm to the station, a cop: no trains running
any longer, she said. I get a standard cop response to why:
orders, I don't know, nothing, nothing. no buses, either.
it's seven or eight miles from bedford park boulevard
to ninety fourth street on the west side of manhattan.
it's hills, it's flats, it's different neighborhoods. I start to walk.

v

I bum my first cigarette in two years off a workman
at lehman college, a tasteless double filter piece of string I soon stubbed
out. beginning to feel like an automaton. unreality is
following behind me, hiding when i turn around. that feeling grows
as I go on. on sedgwick, I pass a con edison truck.
the driver did a hey buddy, he has a tv in there. I go in, see
the tower falling, no accident. the scene is playing over and over and over.
                                        I will see that scene a
thousand times. each time it will do
the very same thing to me. the very same thing.
i left the truck. I reach fordham road via sedgwick avenue; no
longer a hill or a street, but a parking lot, cops are at the bridge.
no vehicular traffic is allowed into manhattan. unreality becomes me.

vi

I eased by the police, their lights, their cars. they aren't looking.
drivers on their way into the bronx pull up to ask
and I tell them they can leave, but they can't get back.
one driver believes me, and turns his suv around,
others continue on. some seem bothered by disruptions to their plans.
inwood valley is dominican now, and the radios were blasting in spanish:
bodegas, repair shops, travel agencies, liquor stores
I could have stopped to ask the latest, but I thought I was dying, too.

vii

and I didn't stop, couldn't stop. I had to go on. I had to get home.
I struck up a conversation with some guy walking alongside me
but he disappeared in a crowd. no singing in the churches. no bells.
except for the hordes walking against me, coming from downtown,
everything was as it might always have been: busy, busy streets,
busier than usual. but quiet. even the cars clogging broadway.
I passed the hospital. I passed the spot the audubon ballroom used to be.
where malcom died. I thought of jeannie and rhoda, who lived
down the block, thirteen when I was thirteen.

viii
at the trinity cemeteries, on one fifty fifth
the first bus came slowly by.
I may have looked dead; the driver stopped the bus;
he refused to take fares, we rode,
the doors open, anyone who wanted on got on.
I rode the bus to one hundred tenth,
where it turned east and I walked south.
on ninety ninth, i stopped for take out. it was no good,
I drank. the tv was on.

ix
by the time I got home, it had all been done. two planes.
two towers. the dead uncounted. the dust rolling towards all. the towers
                                              down. it played
over and over again.

x
over and over again.

Rodney Pybus
Three Hoopoes in a Drawer

I promise – no sliding panels, no mirrors! Come on – have a good look!
I open the top drawer and (under the retired mauve socks
marked '*Will Power*' from Stratford-on-Avon) reveal two inches
of smoked vermilion sealing wax, a scrawled Fifties postcard from Soho
reading **Big Chest for Sale**, half a wing off a tortoiseshell, and then

making a forced march into the hinterland with no compass, I come up with
a whole farmyard – somewhere near Aspatria under a muddy, long-suffering
afternoon sky, waiting for the late Sheila Fell and her palette of umber
                                                            and slate.
Too early, wrong farm. Next, a pizza scoffed outside *The Golden Dragon*
                                                            in 1977.
That would have been Palm Beach. I mean, the one in New South Wales.
Blue water by Hockney. And now the air is fluttering by my left ear
from the deckle-edged vowels of a lovely Wienerin of a certain age:
we are dancing, cheekily, at her house in Gloriettegasse… and we are speaking
of her moody daughter and her daggering, that is to say, poignant, black looks
just because I'm hugging her *soignée* and very sufficient mother – Frau Siedek
likes this, she tells me, warmly… but before anything more educational
                                                            can occur

I find myself with a lucid arrangement of marble, a sea like aubergine,
and a ripe persimmon sun on its slow way down from heaven
over Apollo's temple at Sounion – I'd better see if it's still there,
the wretched John Smith's autograph, incised in 1810. Touch and go. *Touch
and go!* That's the rule. Suddenly there are Greek connections
whizzing everywhere, particles and pronouns from the past, whatevers
that shake you dizzy with discovery, like the hoopoe king I came across
                                                            in my teens
in a comedy by someone even funnier than God. Since then

I've had this craving for a glimpse of your *echt* hoopoe, an exotic in
pancake make-up with excitable crest, and a couple of old-fashioned
Newcastle United wings. No luck for half a life-time... It's true, *Tereu!*
But now, this late summer day, I've opened the drawer – *et voilà*:

                                                        three hoopoes
feeding in a French paddock, decurving bills picking over the earth like
proof-readers who've lost their specs, still busy with the syntax of grass...
The pleasure comes with a rush and a grin, with a call of *hoo-poo-poo*
and the magpie kit, and who would not then put their hands together
for the shade of the great *maestro* Aristophanes?

Good that they take no notice of the brat on his coughing two-stroke
or the old dobbin plodging and squelching the field to clarts, or me,

                                                        staring –
I stare till my eyes begin to dribble from deep inside with the delighted

                                                        pain
that pirouettes round such a moment – so many times, past recollection,
I have found this drawer empty, all the birds flown without so much
as testing the air with fresh musics, the landscape bitter and sere, as we
used to say. And now? Trust me, they're here, I tell you, they're here.
Don't go and startle them with your disbelief –

CENTREFOLD

… and Mystery is what apprentices seek to be trained in.

—Sean O'Brien

Poet and Translator: a dialogue

SASHA DUGDALE AND RUTH FAINLIGHT

When we began this dialogue we touched on various themes: our motivations for translation; the relationship between writing our own poems and translating others; how we came to translation and how it affects our own poetry. As the dialogue found its shape, it grew beyond these themes into a general examination of our thoughts and feelings about poetry.

Sasha: For me, translation is a duty, a job. I take the children to school, come home and begin translating. I can work at translation in the way I imagine other people work at prose. In that respect it is very different from poetry, which occupies me as and when it wishes, and frequently not at all (although a poem which has already been conceived can be worked on in this less whimsical way, and, indeed, should be). But translation is also a duty because I feel some sense of obligation to translate. Whenever I visit Russia I find so much that I feel we should know about in Britain. The Russian writers I want to translate deserve to have our readership and we deserve to hear them. I am also burdened by a more abstract sense of duty. There is literature out there which has the power to convince people how similar the human spirit is, despite its many cultural forms. However lofty that may sound, I don't think it has ever been more relevant than it is just at the moment: the better the translation, the more unsettling the sensation that the writer is sitting at our shoulder in a completely different world.

I have begun here, with the duty of it, because translation earns me my keep, and I spend most of my working life with a dictionary and a Russian text spread in front of me.

Ruth: I don't seem to have such a 'socially responsible' attitude to translation! But at those times when I can only sit blankly in front of an empty sheet of paper, with no ideas or inspiration, no 'tune' in my head, a very effective way to escape that demoralised mood is through translation. Giving a poem the close attention necessary to understand it – there is no better way to read than as a possible translator – is a technique I can usually rely on to change my state of mind and even possibly open the door to my own poetry. Sometimes, the effort to inhabit the mind and emotions of the other poet, indeed to become the other poet, can cut through the Gordian knot of my own numbness. The problem presented by a poem – how to convey its particular form and shape and vocabulary, the choice of words used by the other poet, what they mean and what I can do in an attempt to create another artefact with other material (another language, English) which might produce something like the same effect on the reader – is irresistible, even though I am quite aware that it can never be fully solved. Dryden's definition of translation is, "to produce the text which the foreign poet would have written had he been composing in one's own tongue."

Perhaps the entire poem should be regarded as the equivalent of an extended idiomatic phrase. Idioms are the oldest and most vital strata of any language, its true soul and natural poetry, and the translation of idioms has always been a case of finding equivalents rather than of word-for-word translation – of empathy and the inspired guess. The 'other' poem must be remade into another language. I read it again and again, until the sound pattern comes clear and I feel I understand the aural relationship between the words and lines. I think about the poem as a statement: what exactly, in the most precise and profound sense, does the poet want it to say? How many different layers of meaning can be extracted from it? Next, I consider the images which have been chosen to illustrate that meaning, and the connections of sound and subject matter between those images, until I feel that I am as near to the original inspiration as sympathy and imagination allow. If, by a combination of luck and humility, I am able to enter the enclosed world of the poem and look out from it through its creator's eyes, then words and images begin to crystallise in my own mind. The poem I want to translate has begun to inspire me.

Translation can be seen as the activity of reading carried to its logical extreme. Printed words are a code which must be deciphered to be understood, and every reader participates actively in the creative process. Those black marks on paper enter the brain, to be taken apart and reassembled on the basis of already existing material in each reader's memory, his or her deciphering ability. The contours that shape my mountains can never be exactly the same as those which shape the mountains you visualise when you read the word 'mountain'. This working association between writer and reader differentiates literature from drama and film, where every character and image is fixed by the tangible reality of an actor's presence or the director's concept. But there is no way to check whether my interpretation of a group of words, or idea of a person or place, is the same as yours – no final tribunal to pronounce on which is right. Perhaps this ultimate, tantalising uncertainty is what makes the relationship so close.

Sasha: I want to respond to the point you make about the difference between literature and theatre or film. I translate both plays and poetry and I have come to my own understanding of how genre affects translation. When I translate a poem I aim to recreate as far as possible the relationship between each word and the vast cultural world each word draws in its thrall. So the words are the players: they should remain uninflected, they should retain their depth and ambiguity of character. Plays are different. In practice a translator is one link in a long chain stretching from writer to viewer. My job is to pass the play on with as little of its integrity lost as possible. This means reaching conclusions about relationships and characters and reviving these as best I can in English lines. The director Simon Usher once said to me that when poets read their poems they do so in an open and unresolved way, allowing every word full play in the line. When actors read poems they inflect them, because their training dictates that they come to an understanding of the poem and convey that understanding. My theory is that in the theatre texts are inflected to allow greater ambiguity and openness at a different level: the level of relationships and dramatic incident. This affects the practice of theatre translation.

℘

Ruth: When a new poem presents itself, the first indication is always through sound, the tune I hear in my head, even before I have heard or understood the words that carry it. And when I am translating, the first thing I must do is find the 'tune' of the poet's voice. The work of each poet has its own tune, as individual as fingerprints, and each language has its basic sound. As much as poems in my own language, the totally different rhythms and sounds of poems in another can jolt me awake. Iambic pentameter is not the only tune!

My state of mind when translating a poem from another language is similar to that when working on a poem of my own; it is the same journey, but in the opposite direction. The words are already there, yet they are not the right words. The two have the relationship to each other of a photograph to its negative. Whatever triggers the process, I become aware that already there is a tangled knot of ideas and feelings in my mind, crucially involved with the particular words embodying and expressing them. It is obvious that 'poetry work' has been going on for some time, but in a region of the mind not accessible to examination or direct influence. These first words are the poem's living matter, and putting them onto paper is tricky and delicate and messy, like brain surgery, or delivering a baby. Not one healthy cell must be hurt; the child has to be brought out alive and undamaged. Conscious and unconscious powers are being drawn on. I concentrate my attention onto what are still only half-emerged intimations of sounds and images, open my inner ear to the poem's melody already announcing itself – rhythmically throbbing on a level more basic than that of the particular words. I note down whatever occurs to me, every word that attaches itself to those sounds, and the images cohering to them like weeds clinging to dredged-up treasure. I must be careful not to reject anything. Because I do not yet understand its importance, the one word inadvertently discarded at this stage might be the vital node from which the poem will grow – as is so beautifully said in Psalm 118: "The stone which the builders refused is become the head stone of the corner." And sooner or later, I must try to assess this discovered, or recovered, material with all the objectivity and intelligence I can muster. Often I am surprised by what I read, as though it had been written by someone else. This is when the process of writing my own poem and translating the poem of another writer come closest together.

Sasha: I often wonder about the combination of poetry and translation. In Russia it is an accepted tradition. Poets who were not able to write openly or publish during Soviet times turned to translation – Pasternak, Akhmatova, Mandel'shtam, all, I think, published far more translations than original poems in their lifetimes. As a result the Russian tradition of poetry translation is a very particular one. As one Russian writer put it, "the translator is the slave of prose and the rival of the poem." (The Russian translator Marina Boroditskaya said jokingly that the *male* Russian translator will rush to translate something someone else has just translated in order to flaunt his own creative powers, whereas the *female* Russian translator will look for something different to translate, in the spirit of economy.) Poetic skill is rated over strict accuracy, and the translator is poet, first and foremost.

I fight this in myself. Or at least I fight the dishonesty of writing poetry at the expense of another's conceived poem. I can't define this dishonesty, although I know it in myself. Apart from perceiving departures from the text to be a moral failing, I find that my own deviations from the original metaphor and idiom are usually the weakest points in the poem. When I replace them with the original the freshness and rightness of it startles me. There is a discipline in translation which yields better creative results and I have wondered how to harness this to the less predictable, but equally technical business of writing poetry.

Almost unconsciously I began to write poems in the voices of others. Perhaps I wondered somewhere in my mind whether I couldn't use the principle of translation to observe and record the lives and thoughts of other creative people. I began by writing a series of poems about Turner. I don't know why I chose Turner. It seemed an almost arbitrary choice, a snippet of information on a label at an exhibition. But I liked that – it was almost thrust upon me, in the way most of my translations are: an initially unpromising, closed box, which yields all sorts of things, and eventually, as I sift through them, some common thread, a moment of enlightenment.

Most of the playwrights I translate are men, and most of the personae I have adopted have been men. I talked to Sinéad Morrissey about this – she has written an extraordinary poem in the voice of the prison reformer John Howard. I think we agreed that there was a sneaky sense of redress in ventriloquizing powerful male figures in history, not to mention the benefits of distance between the poet and the poem: freedom to be utterly other, no possible biographical reading.

I want to illustrate this with a poem. I wrote this sonnet about Turner, who is distraught when his father dies. But in fact the poem itself disguises a translation. I have longed to translate a poem by Pushkin which begins, "It is time, my friend, it is time, / the heart asks for peace". This in turn disguises the autobiographical. I wanted to find a way of expressing the relationship between personal melancholy and creative resilience in an English poem.

Turner at Petworth

My Father died Thank you, you are kind.
Three years have passed and still it makes me weep.
He was the best factotum I could find;
He could stretch the perfect canvas in his sleep.
A wigmaker by trade, he lived by cutting hair.
Soft it fell, like snow, about his feet.
As a boy I remember how the air
Was scented with pomade and tasted sweet.

And now he's gone. I am boring you, I fear.
And now he's gone. It's not a terrible despair –
Just the sense of passing time, year on year,
And one becomes so suddenly aware
Of slowly dying. It's more than one can bear:
I paint a halo now on every head of hair.

Sometimes, it worries me that I would be unable to make anything of an open field, a vast and endless choice of themes and feelings. Does translation

way? There is something addictive about standing behind someone else, wearing someone else's mask. What exactly is the relationship between one's own writing and translating others? If poetry really is the product of idleness, then translation must surely be its enemy, I think, as I squirrel away at a poem translation.

Our own traditions of translation seem to reinforce my intuition. I know few poets who are also professional translators. They do exist – you, David Constantine and George Szirtes are notable examples – but on the whole translation has slipped onto the wrong side in the schism between 'poet' and 'pedant'. I don't imagine it is a lack of linguistic ability, more the sense that these occupations are not naturally compatible.

Ruth: About the schism between poets and translation, I must disagree with you. Certainly Elaine Feinstein, with her superb translations of Marina Tsvetaeva – and, to choose almost at random, the French translations of Stephen Romer – are other equally notable examples of first-rate English poets as translators. And there are too many excellent American poets whose translations from a variety of languages have enriched our knowledge of poetry from every part of the world, for me even to try to list them. Thinking about this difference between attitudes to translation – if indeed there is one – I wonder if it might have some connection to the fact that most Americans, whether or not they are poets, are more likely to have had direct personal contact with other languages through their immediate families: the grandmother or uncle who spoke Italian or Spanish or Lithuanian or Chinese or Yiddish or one of a score of other languages, than has been the case for the notoriously monolingual British! Perhaps in another generation or two, poets from immigrant communities in England will be so integrated into this society that they will begin to translate not only the literature of their origins, but from any language they choose.

Spanish, not French, was the standard second language in American schools, and when I arrived in England at the age of fifteen, it was the only modern language I had studied. During my twenties I lived in Spain for four years. I love the noble sound of spoken Spanish. This should explain why most of my translations have been from that language – although in 1987 I did publish, in the USA, the first book to appear in English of the poems of the Portuguese poet, Sophia de Mello Breyner. In the 1960s I discovered the work of Cesar Vallejo, and the only way to understand what he was doing seemed through translation. Also in that decade, Alan Sillitoe and I collaborated on a version of Lope de Vega's *Fuenteovejuna*, which was published under the title, *All Citizens Are Soldiers.* During the past few years I have translated the work of several Latin American poets – Blanca Varela from Peru, Maria Negroni from Argentina, Yolanda Pantin from Venezuela. I have just finished a sequence of poems by the Mexican poet Elsa Cross, and am now translating another Mexican poet, Victor Manuel Mendiola. I have also translated from French and, like many others, from languages of which I have very little or no knowledge – such as Russian and classical Greek – something which only becomes possible with the help of native speakers, and 'cribs'. A current translation project involves working from cribs. My partner in this is Robert Littman, an American professor of Classics. Because he admired my Sibyl poems, he suggested that we collaborate on a new translation of Sophocles' Theban Plays. He provided me with detailed literals, and many notes, and it seems to have worked. I have completed *Oedipus Rex*, and if all goes well, we shall continue with the trilogy.

Translating poetry has made me realise how fortunate I am to have English as my mother tongue. Writing my own poems or translating others, more and more I appreciate the richness of this wonderful medium: its enormous, rich, specific vocabulary and the blessed flexibility of its structures.

Sasha: Translation is a form of restoration, a craft. I like the economy of the craft, and I like the fact that little goes to waste in translation. A Russian poet once told me her metaphor for translation: a joke about a policeman who found a decapitated head on the pavement. The policeman wrote, "Head found on pav… pav… pavm…", then, unable to spell "pavement", he kicked the head onto the road: "Head found on road". In my metaphor the policeman would have picked the head up and taken it with him. But that is to return to your quote about the head stone of the corner, Ruth.

I try to remain as close to the text as I possibly can. I spend hours shuffling words around, like pieces in those little picture-puzzles, where you can only shift a single piece at a time. I occupy myself with absurd questions, like "what iambic word describes a bittern's call?" I have been working on a sequence of poems by Elena Shvarts about Rome. I haven't been to Rome, so I spent long hours looking at photographs of the main squares and attractions, so I too could imagine Gogol tripping down the Spanish Steps… I like to feel confident in the space around the poem, to know the world from which it came, even if I do then attempt to keep very close to the original. Translation reaches into the rest of my life: the text I am translating has for a while the run of my thoughts and my imagination and for better or for worse I am bound to the writer and the writer's vision.

Ruth: And here is a poem from *Moon Wheels*, my new collection, which (this thought has just occurred to me) is as much a description of translating poetry as of writing a poem:

Mosaic

Writing a poem, shifting
words from there to here
is like choosing between
hexagons of tile
for a mosaic, or the next
move in a game of chess.

The final image is clear
in my mind – now abstract
as the Alhambra, then
complex as Ravenna –
kaleidoscope,
jewelled tiara.

But which piece goes
where, which words cohere
– unknowable until
the riddle's solved, the circle
closed, the pattern fixed –
the poem exact.

Books in translation by Dugdale and Fainlight include:

Sasha Dugdale:
Russian: *Plasticine*, Vassily Sigarev (Nick Hern Books, 2002)
Terrorism Presnyakov Brothers (Nick Hern Books, 2003)
Ladybird, Vassily Sigarev (Nick Hern Books, 2004)
Life Without, Selected Poetry and Prose, Tatiana Shcherbina (Bloodaxe Books, 2004)

Ruth Fainlight:
French: Selection of poems by Jean Joubert included in Fainlight's *Selected Poems*
(Sinclair-Stevenson, 1995)
Portuguese: *Navigations*, Sophia de Mello Breyner (Casa da Moeda, Portugal, 1983)
Marine Rose, Sophia de Mello Breyner (Black Swan USA, 1987)
Spanish: Play: *All Citizens Are Soldiers* (with Alan Sillitoe) Lope de Vega (Macmillan, 1966).
Selections of poems by Sophia de Mello Breyner, Elsa Cross, Victor Manuel Mendiola, Maria
Negroni, Cesar Vallejo and Sophocles to be included in *Moon Wheels* (Bloodaxe Books, 2006)

Rilke and the Contemporary Reader

SEAN O'BRIEN

One charge that could justifiably be laid against much contemporary poetry in the British Isles is that it is indulgently anecdotal. There seem to be two kinds of anecdotalism at large, with more than one source. One (often found among older poets) is the degenerate phase of a kind of writing traceable to Larkin, inclined to the proverbial without Larkin's selectiveness or formal memorability; the other (whose exponents are on the whole younger) owes much to Frank O'Hara as filtered through Huddersfield. Both kinds trade on an attachment to authenticity which is felt to outbid both technical reach and thematic scale. Both serve a misconceived 'democratic' notion of poetry as entertainment, in which equality (a notion misplaced in this context) emerges not in diversity but as sameness. These problems are mirrored among the avant-garde, where the pleasure principle is tirelessly punished. One might almost suspect that among some writers there is a strange underlying antipathy towards language itself. In one sense, given that very little work from any period of poetry survives, this hardly matters; but it does suggest a widespread lack of imaginative confidence. At the same time, some of the most interesting contemporary poets are powerfully drawn to the work of a modern poet who was prepared to stake everything on the imagination's resources.

Since his work was translated into English by Leishman and Spender, Rainer Maria Rilke (1875–1926) has never lost his popularity with English-speaking poets and readers. The "Santa Claus of loneliness" appealed to Auden, to Lowell in *Imitations* and to Randall Jarrell. More generally, a certain recognizable, religiose tone and an atmosphere of yearning have long been installed in American poetry, for good or ill. Poets as different as Louise Glück and Jorie Graham show clear affinities with Rilke, while legions of inferiors are, we might say, emotionally imitative of the German poet. Translations of Rilke accumulate steadily, among them those by C. F. MacIntyre, M. D. Herter Norton, Michael Hamburger, Stephen Mitchell and Stephen Cohn. There is nothing surprising in this, perhaps: Rilke is clearly a major modern poet, so it is natural for poets and translators turn to his work, and for the readership of poetry, insofar as one exists, to do the same.

Yet it seems that interest in Rilke is undergoing a phase of intensification at present. To speak only of Britain and Ireland, 2002 saw Jo Shapcott's *Tender Taxes*, her versions of the poems which Rilke wrote in French towards the end of his life; Michael Hamburger's *An Unofficial Rilke* (1980) was republished as *Turning Point: Miscellaneous Poems 1912-1926* in 2003. *Faint Harps and Silver Voices* (2000), the selected translations of Hamburger's long-standing collaborator Christopher Middleton, naturally included a solid representation of Rilke. Don Paterson is soon to publish a version of the *Sonnets to Orpheus*; Seamus Heaney has recently published translations from the sonnets in the *TLS*; Robert Saxton's *Manganese* (2003) contains versions of ten of them. Robin Robertson included 'Falling', a fine version of the 1902 poem 'Autumn', in *Slow Air* (2002); Rilkean angels occur in the work of W. N. Herbert. There would be no shortage of other examples. For some years Michael Hofmann has been preparing *Rilke in English*, an anthology of translations by many hands in the Penguin Classics series, scheduled for publication in 2007 and setting Rilke alongside writers of founding importance in European literature such as Virgil, Horace and Dante. If you can find a poetry section in a bookshop nowadays, it is likely to include more than one selection of Rilke's work. Could the same be said of Valéry, whom Rilke considered "the one nearest to me among the poets of my generation", his peer among his contemporaries, and the poet whose work he credited with breaking several years' stalemate in the composition of the *Duino Elegies*? Only demand, or a sure sense of its imminence, can explain Rilke's prominence. This is especially striking when we consider how little modern and contemporary German literature is readily available in Britain, despite Hofmann's heroic rate of output of new translations of fiction. Even the place of Thomas Mann's novels appears to be at risk on the shelves of Waterstone's among the three-for-two banalities.

How are we to account for the phenomenon of Rilke's appeal? It may of course simply be that there are interesting translations available. Among these is the work of some leading poets who are not trained linguists but who are drawn to approach Rilke because of his peculiar power to engage the reader. Jo Shapcott has asked:

> The fascination for poets [...] is it that Rilke's poems demand both that you pour yourself into them, and that you open yourself to them in a way that makes the act of reading more like writing – or, at least, some connected experience like conversing, touching, praying? The relationship of the reader to these poems is unlike any other I can think of.

Perhaps "praying" is a little worrying (for reasons I'll return to below), but

Shapcott is surely right to suggest that the *address* of Rilke's poems – sometimes involving "you", often using "we" to active effect rather than as mere rhetorical reinforcement – does work to implicate the reader as a companion of a sort, a privileged listener rather than an accidental passer-by or a punter who pays on the door. This has something to do with the peculiarly privileged status which Rilke spent much of his time engineering and sustaining. To Rilke's admirers during his lifetime, that European pariah of rich women and compliant publishers, his appeal was often that of a prophet, an emissary from a higher power. The archangel in a suit had a more-than-literary function, one markedly apparent even in a culture where literature was often required to operate at a visionary degree of elevation. Even so, Rilke's role retained a strong personal dimension, as his vast and meticulous correspondence suggests. And the poems clearly reach beyond a supportive coterie. With their combination of scale, exhilarating and eerie perception, and their marked respect and courtesy towards the reader, they make it hard to resist the attempt to translate them, though numerous honourable examples testify to the extreme difficulty of the task. It seems too that the most interesting translations are often the most boldly interventionist, and there is a precedent for this in Rilke's own practice. In his translations of Valéry, as his biographer Donald Prater expresses it, Rilke retained the "outward form of the verses: yet his images are often subtly different, and the thought sometimes elusively changed, resulting in a German poem with a beauty of its own but going beyond translation in the strict sense – 'as if a piece written for the harpsichord were played on an organ.'"

There may be less desirable features to the attraction Rilke is exerting; or perhaps it would be more accurate to say, in some of the meanings that are projected on to him. This negative potential is glancingly apparent in an American context. In his essay 'Trafficking in the Radiant: The Spiritualization of American Poetry', published in the July/August 2005 edition of *American Poetry Review*, the critic Ira Sadoff noted that "In the past two decades, Rilke has replaced Neruda as one of our most influential poets" – the political surreal displaced by romantic prophecy, perhaps. Sadoff juxtaposes this with a renewed interest in Eliot, as evidence of a reactionary evasiveness at work in American culture in general (although, as in Britain, poetry hardly registers on the cultural instruments there). He diagnoses an attempt by some to escape from our fraught times, an attempt which plays into the hands of an increasingly prescriptive and monolithic religious-political Right, whose apocalyptic visions are founded on precisely the materialism which some are fleeing in order to join the more fiery Protestant churches.

Sadoff has little time for things of the spirit, and not much more – in this essay at any rate – for poems themselves. He quotes a garrulous but compassionate piece of residual Catholicism by W. S. DiPiero and damns its presumptuous sympathy and submissiveness. Then, turning to T. S. Eliot, he argues:

> In Eliot's anti-Semitism, the Jew becomes his threatening object of desire: his projective identification of Jews as representing the body, externalizing his feelings of guilt and shame onto the material body of the Jew, originates in his longing to transcend the body and the world: the implication of which is that the body is a source of debasement, sin and decay.

Sadoff may well be right in his formulation. Certainly the problem of Eliot's loathsome attitudes – or Pound's – is never going to be talked away as a mere unfortunate characteristic of the times. Yet the quoted example provides a rather unsatisfying way of reading poems, since it converts them from events into summaries. In doing so it excludes the three-dimensional dramatic life which is so important in drawing us to poetry in the first place, and which – though not for Eliot in this case, it would appear – is also the source of its frequent opposition to received ideas and prejudices. Sadoff intends to dispute the truth-content of his examples, but he's actually opposed to what he infers the poets *feel* – about the suffering of others, about Jews. As Rilke wrote in *The Notebook of Malte Laurids Brigge*: "Poetry isn't, as people imagine, merely feelings (these come soon enough); it is experiences." One can agree with Sadoff's interpretation while also thinking that there must be more to the poetry in the first place if it is to deserve greater literary attention than the ravings of a neo-Fascist website.

What exactly might Rilke signify in the terms Sadoff sets out? It seems reasonable to suggest that the metaphysical cast of Rilke's imagination exerts a strong attraction when Christianity – arguably doomed from the moment it began to defend and reform itself in the light of secular pressures – may be in terminal decline in Europe as a whole. Rilke, a lapsed Catholic whose religious views were predictably idiosyncratic, is perhaps felt to meet a spiritual need or aspiration without requiring adherence to an explicit dogma. For example, he finds room for sexuality where Christianity is still often hobbled by shame. Indeed, he sees sexuality as an aspect of necessity:

> Again and again, though we know the landscape of love
> and the little graveyard with its lamenting names

and the terrible reticent gorge, in which the others
end: again and again we go out in couples
under the ancient trees, lie down again and again
among the wild flowers, facing the sky.

(Translated by Michael Hamburger.)

Rilke also privileges the interior life, which has a powerful appeal in a
time of widespread political exhaustion and despair, when many people fear
that the democratic state may either have run its course or be facing
extinction at the hands of those elected to sustain it. To some this must seem
like an evasion. To others it will be essential to try to take the measure of life
in terms subtler than those allowed by the widespread impoverishment of
language and argument which seems to accompany the gradual closing of
the circle of state control: after all, what are we claiming to be civilized *about*?
Rilke (who himself seems to have lacked any power of sustained political
attention) insists that there is more to life than what we see or directly
experience, and that what appears negative – in particular, death itself –
needs to be grasped as part of a larger whole.

If these are among the reasons for Rilke's appeal, then we may be in
dangerous territory. For all that Rilke deliberately and painfully and with
complete seriousness sacrificed himself, and others, and much else besides,
to his work and to the (by no means immutable) convictions it embodies,
the ideas associated with him are problematic because their borders with
wishfulness and sentimentality are conspicuously insecure. We live in a
period of designer religion and low-cost spirituality, when profundity is
another product to be bought off the shelf. A New Age Rilke would not be
Rilke at all, of course, and there is nothing to be said to readers who might
seek to adapt him to this end. It should be acknowledged, though, that
serious-minded Anglophone readers too have often found the spiritual
climate of the *Duino Elegies* and the *Sonnets to Orpheus* unpalatable, partly
because of the work's blithe indifference to potential accusations of
pretension and partly because there is little precisely comparable material in
the English tradition (Rilke himself in return shows a corresponding lack of
interest in English poetry). A reputation for otherworldliness, for having
'gone beyond', for table tapping and gauzy imprecision, clings to Rilke, but
this is misleading. There is in fact no point in reading Rilke in order to *evade*
the world: however rarefied the climate into which his work led him, it was
clearly part of *this* world – hence the steady focus on death – and must have
seemed to him pointless otherwise. His great poem 'To Hölderlin'
(September 1914) praises his predecessor for an act of imaginative

restoration. Of Hölderlin's "night landscape" he writes: "No one / Renounced this more nobly and no one / Restored it so nearly intact, or asked for less." The tribute is to a poet who extended the sense of imaginative possibility. In December 1926, in "Komm du, du letzter, den ich anerkenne" ("Now come, the last that I can recognize"), Rilke, dying in extreme pain from leukaemia, described his condition unsparingly:

> ...Ganz rein, ganz planlos frei von Zukunft stieg
> ich auf des Leidens wirren Scheiterhaufen,
> so sicher nirgend Künftiges zu kaufen
> um dieses Herz, darin der Vorrat schwieg.
> Bin ich es noch, der da unkenntlich brennt?
> Erinnerungen reiß ich nicht herein.
> O Leben, Leben: Draußensein.
> Und ich in Lohe. Niemand der mich kennt.

> ...Quite pure of forethought, futureless and free
> I mounted suffering's tangled, criss-crossed pyre,
> so sure there was no purchase to acquire
> for this heart's future, all its store now silent.
> What burns there, so transmuted? Is that I?
> Into this fire I drag no memory.
> To be alive, alive: to be outside.
> And I ablaze. With no one who knows me.

(Translation by Michael Hamburger)

Not an iota of that unique, many-eyed poetic intelligence is allowed to lapse: the personal cry is dramatized in full, seen by the author and known by the reader as an utterance both representative and particular.

And perhaps what draws some very gifted poets to immerse themselves in Rilke's work and to make new versions of it lies in Rilke's insistence that poetry is not something other than poetry. In recent years, as I suggested above, readers could have been forgiven for thinking that some of those involved in poetry actually hate it, whether knowingly or not – in some cases by ignoring the demands of technique and in others by excluding the aesthetic from an arid and repetitive poetry-as-critique. In his witty and wide-ranging Defence of Poetry, given as the T. S. Eliot lecture, 'The Dark Art of Poetry', Don Paterson argued that "the insistence on poetry's auxiliary usefulness – for example in raising issues of cultural identity, as a form of therapy, or generating academic papers [...] has encouraged it to think far less of itself, and so eroded its real power to actually inspire readers to think or live differently." In passing, Paterson seems to overstate the case against criticism (derided as "academic papers"). He is not alone, apparently. In 1903 Rilke wrote in the first of his *Letters to a Young Poet* (and was later to repeat):

> there is nothing which touches works of art so little as does the language of criticism [...] Few things are in fact as accessible to reason or to language as people will generally try to make us us believe. Most phenomena are *unsayable*, and have their being in a dimension which no word has ever entered; and works of art are the most unsayable of all – they are mysterious presences whose lives endure alongside our own perishable lives.

This kind of thing seems guaranteed to provoke the irritated scorn of many Anglophones: a precious up-itself-ness which throws out a real point – the integrity of the work of art – along with a bathful of richly-scented posturing and spilt religion. Rilke's contention, though, is at bottom wholly serious, and in fact very close to Paterson's: the work of art, the poem, has its own imaginative life. To approach it as merely a version of something that already exists – for example, as a highly decorated or elaborated commonplace – is to lose the chance of contact with it. Rilke himself was embarrassed by his own academic unreadiness, finding systematic reading a torture, and was at times inclined, like many poets outside the academy, to pull rank by ascending a secret staircase to The Truth. But this is not to dispose of criticism. Literature cannot function in the absence of reflection, or of readers who respond to the complexity of the original work with a corresponding quality of attention. The challenge for critics is to find language which is neither posthumous Mandarin, nor a sealed tunnel of ideological anxiety, nor the fleeting chatter of the times. In the case of Rilke this involves, clearly, a strong sense of the dramatic, of the poem as a process whose gaze is often in large part directed to the future.

The force of "Now come, the last that I can recognize", where no personal future remains, arises partly from the fact that for Rilke death has been not only the inescapable human fate but also a kind of moral / imaginative imprimatur. To hold such a belief is one thing; to test what Empson called "the trigger of the literary man's biggest gun" in the event itself is another. A comment by Michael Hamburger on an earlier phase of Rilke's work is also applicable to its end: "Rilke's personal confessions and his existential affirmations or negations are inseparable from questions about the function of poetry and poets." To live was for Rilke to be writing, or thinking about it, or, in the case of the *Duino Elegies*, waiting for years on end for a particular imaginative opportunity to re-present itself. Vocation is hardly a strong enough word for this commitment. There is no evasion in Rilke's lines on facing death, any more than in Keats's address to Fanny Brawne. It is understandable that translation does not wholly capture the tone of: "O Leben, Leben: Draußensein", where memory, longing, agony, acceptance and understanding are all simultaneously present. The lyric power of the piece depends on a lifetime of intelligence applied to making poems.

That intelligence enabled Rilke to move happily among language which in other hands might have seemed inert and abstract: it seems as though what Hamburger calls Rilke's "virtuosity of feeling" enables him to lend substance to terms which the contemporary reader in English may at first be inclined to reject, for example from *Sonnets to Orpheus*: Grief, Triumph and Yearning, all personified; the Unsayable; permanence, the heart, not-being, destiny, the Earth. At the same time, natural imagery – wind, earth, roots, the rose and so on – is continually employed for philosophical ends without (and this is the intriguing part) losing its original valency. The rose never feels like a token or a surface pretext but is, rather, charged with an interior light. Concrete and abstract coexist successfully, partly, one suspects, because of Rilke's evident command of tone, gesture and timing, partly because such a practice remained a live possibility in German.

When Rilke completed the *Duino Elegies* (published 1923), Anglo-American modernism had been cleansing the stables of exhausted romanticism and its attendant parochialism, trying at once to restore precision to language and to renew its power of connotation. William Carlos Williams spoke of his objections to Eliot and Pound's recourse to Europe and of his desire for "no ideas but in things", but Rilke's work, though it approaches the matter from a quite different direction, is also concerned with the inseparability of ideas and things. Where Williams seems to have sought to subordinate ideas (for which read abstractions) to the dramatizing power of a poetry rooted in speech, Rilke moved to abolish the distinction between concrete and abstract by dint of imaginative inclusiveness (which sounds a little like Eliot's myth of the unified sensibility, a gift apparently lost by the time of the English Civil War). The concentration on the particular in the *Neue Gedichte* is not, of course, undertaken purely for its own sake, though its subjects – the Panther, the Cathedral, the Angel, the Merry Go Round – have their own existence, but to refresh and clarify contact between the inner and outer worlds, to provide "a more convincing, more powerful name" for the poet's internal response. By the *Sonnets to Orpheus* the act of naming through poetry has become a means of both bridging and acknowledging the distance between the inner and outer, a kind of celebration of tragedy, a drama of redemptive knowledge, an affirmation of imaginative power, by virtue of which the very existence of the unattainable ensures a triumph for the imagination:

> Singe die Gärten, mein Herz, die du nicht kennst; wie in Glas
> eingegossene Gärten klar, unerreichbar.
> Wasser und Rosen von Ispahan oder Schiras,
> singe sie selig, preise sie, keinem vergleichbar.
>
> Zeige, mein Herz, daß du niehmals entbehrst.
> Daß sie dich meinen, ihre reifenden Feigen.
>
> 2, XXI

This is rendered by Stephen Cohn as:

> O sing, my heart, the gardens you know not – they are as
> gardens poured into glass; clear, unattainable.
> water, roses of Isfahan, of Shiraz,
> sing them, delight in them, all incomparable.
>
> Prove, O my heart, that you cannot live without them,
> that their figs ripening now ripen for you [...]

Although Cohn has provided some of the most interesting and readable Rilke translations, especially of the *Duino Elegies*, here the ungrateful pen itches to amend the word order of the first line and to understate the rhythm (which is faithful to the exultant drive of the original) in order to have something to brace the exoticism against – a case in point about interventionism. In the light of this passage, it is useful to note one of the ways Rilke himself commented on the task of writing the *Sonnets to Orpheus*:

> I keep always referring to them as sonnets. They are per-
> haps the freest and most transfigured verse that might be
> understood as belonging to this form – usually so quiet
> and consistent. But it was the very task of transforming
> the sonnet, of picking it up and, as it were, taking it along
> on the run, without destroying it, that was in this instance
> my particular problem and my project.

Allowing for the self-confidence, the excited response to a technical challenge is of a sort that could be found in many poets (though Lowell in particular comes to mind) and it makes it plain that that matter and method are inseparable – a truism, but one frequently denied in practice in contemporary poetry. Cohn, however, reaches a surprising conclusion in introducing his version of the *Sonnets to Orpheus*:

> It is a wonderful and teasing truth that poetry's power of invocation, its music, story, images, illuminations, every-*thing* of real importance, may be owed to the relatively unimportant conventions of rhythm or rhyme.

In that sense, how can these "conventions" be "relatively unimportant"? "Conventions'" of the kind to which Cohn refers only exist in use. And they are not simply passes allowing admission to the building. They are the building. Cohn goes on:

> What seems profoundly true of Rilke is that the best of this poet is to be found in the stuff of the poetry; in the nature of its language and of something almost beyond language, its fabric, cadences and imagery, sound and progression. Not discourse. Mystery.

Cohn's own work as a translator tends to undermine his argument in this instance. His version of *Sonnet 2, XVIII* ('Tänzerin: o du verlegung'), though it takes an odd liberty with the third line quoted, manages to suggest Rilke's extraordinary ability to appear not simply to write about time, but to make it present, to *write time*:

> Aber er trug auch, er trug, den Baum der Ekstase.
> Sind sie nicht seine ruhigen Früchte: der Krug,
> reifend gestreift, und die gereiftere Vase?
>
> Und in den Bildern: ist nicht die Zeichnung geblieben,
> die deiner Braue dunkler Zug
> rasch an die Wandung der eigenen Wendung geschrieben?
>
> And it bore fruit too, the tree of your rapture:
> are not these things its inanimate harvest? – the pitcher
> striped like a gourd, the vase even riper and richer?
> And there are pictures: does not the drawing remain

of your dark eyebrows instantly captured
on the surface prepared by yourself in your turning?

  Anyone devoted to poetry is likely to have experienced the vertiginous feeling of encountering a poem or a passage or a phrase which by means of originality or compression exceeds what it has hitherto seemed possible to say. Some poets are lucky enough to feel a whole imaginative circuit surge into life without deliberate intent. These are mysterious experiences – but not, surely, otherworldly ones. Craft, alertness, long thought, timing, reading, good fortune – all play their part, and Mystery is what apprentices seek to be trained in.

The Michael Hamburger translations quoted here are taken from *Turning Point: Miscellaneous Poems 1912-1926* (Anvil, 2003). The Stephen Cohn translations are from *Sonnets to Orpheus with Letters to a Young Poet* (Carcanet, 2000).

B

Bury
Art Gallery
Museum
+Archives

TheText
Festival

Opening Times
Tuesday-Friday 10-5
Saturday 10-1.30
& Sunday 1-4

Admission Free
Tel: 0161 253 5878
textfestival.com

19 March -
27 November 2005

Challenging the boundaries
between art and poetry

Exhibitions
Commissions
Performances
Workshops
Publications

Event

**The Text of
Maurizio Nannucci**
Talk
Tues 29th November
12.30pm
Bury Art Gallery

Exhibitions

Shaun Pickard
6 August - 16 October
Bury Art Gallery

Different Alphabets
17 September - 27
November
Bury Art Gallery

Maurizio Nannucci
29 October - 8 January
Bury Art Gallery

Bury Art Gallery
Tel: 0161 253 5878

REVIEWS

Perhaps the source of our new politics lies in a new poetics. Are you happy?

—Simon Smith

Slanted

ALISON BRACKENBURY

Sebastian Barker, *The Matter of Europe*, Menard, £5.95, ISBN 1874320535
David Harsent, *Legion*, Faber, £8.99, ISBN 0571228097
Gerard Woodward, *We were Pedestrians*, Chatto & Windus,
£9, ISBN 0701178876

Reviewers should not impose the slant of their own prejudices upon their readers. But I will unwisely reveal that I associate Sebastian Barker's poems with lilies, David Harsent's with fire and darkness, and Gerard Woodward's with the kind of shabby rooms in which such preconceptions ought to be safely hidden.

Sebastian Barker's *The Matter of Europe* is, surprisingly, not a collection of poems, and its heart is not lilies, but lists. There are seven, sidling their way through cosmology, evolution and culture. In theory, I would not even pick up these lists. In practice, the book in my hand mesmerised me, not least by its design. Each list runs slant across the page, with a diagonal flash of white space at its centre: time's arrow, room, as Barker suggests, for readers to add their own reflections.

The book itself stands aslant to poetry. Though the lists duly contain timescales and technical terms, they are a poet's, suspending their final words in space: "The present –" Like poems, they can produce an aftershock of thought. In the 'Cosmological Sketch', how new and narrow is the ledge where men and woodlice huddle, "hominids {8-6m Pliocene}" under a slanted cliff of time. Like poems, they draw together the unexpected. The great Chinese poets, Li Po and Tu Fu, hover directly above the Anglo-Saxon Chronicle. Barker's highly personal "sketches" end with a (fairly comprehensive) list of British poets, "a fragment of a world of poetry during this time".

Though the devil may be in the odd detail of *The Matter of Europe*, the angels are in the appendix, with Barker's passionate exploration of poets and philosophers. The goddess Justice, in a fragment from the Greek poet Parmenides, warns darkly:

> You must learn all things
> both the unwavering heart of persuasive truth
> and the opinions of mortals in which is there is no true trust.

Echoes, deep as those from any poem, start from one sentence by the medieval German preacher Eckhart: "Whatever is touched by time is mortal". The translator Helen Waddell wrote movingly of "the leaf-drift ... of forgotten scholarship". Sebastian Barker's strange and scholarly book is nourishment for a future poem, a leaf-drift for a lily.

There are no lilies in *Legion*. This mortal reviewer's slanted opinion of David Harsent can be trusted for this collection. Its first third deals with the darkest of times, war. The reader, too, is kept at a slant to Harsent's horrors, deprived of the clarity of knowing if a poem is set in Carlisle or Croatia. Poets often treat terrible subjects rawly, achieving pity but not poetry. Harsent is far too strong a poet to do so. The many voices and forms of his war poems are carefully worked, with their own formidable armoury of stanza and rhyme.

Even Harsent, I think, cannot quite escape the curse of the modern poetry sequence, which spreads even the best poet's power too thinly. But *Legion* does maintain certain strengths across its battalions. Its names have the music of myth, "the Street of Songs", "the Street of Locks". Its animals are a casual, recurring terror, "heading south to the guns and the promise of fresh meat" ('Filofax').

Poetry is a slant art. Harsent's most menacing poems are his most indirect and musical. 'Harp Strings' is the hinted story of a sudden attack. Subtly, the "silver-grey" of birches slips to hard consonants in "the steel of their side-arms". The long lines are, to the end, haunted by one rhyme:

we were wrong
to see nothing dark in the rain. All this has gone into song.

This formidable poet's strongest work, rightly, mistrusts art.

I mistrust the book's central section, where slabs of neat prose mimic standing stones. But, in *Legion*'s final, single poems, Harsent is at his strongest. His hypnotic intensity sounds in 'The Woman and the Hare': "Now she cuts a mad caper, her body a taper, yes, her body burning". His range animates 'At the Bedside', passing from a dying woman, her body "the dancing particles of space", to a long whispering last line where foreign girls look at their reflection in a train window: "and set themselves softly, sadly, cheek to cheek". No reader who looks for fire in poetry would be disappointed in *Legion*.

No slant of prejudice caused my disappointment with parts of Gerard Woodward's *We were Pedestrians*. I entirely approve of rubbish bins and rawl-plugs as subjects for poetry. But, in Woodward's opening lines –

> My father's industry
> Was too soft for words

– I sense a technical softness which plagues some interior, domestic poems in this collection, where short lines lack weight and final lines trail into "might" and "almost", bereft of verbs.

Woodward is a different and quietly vigorous poet once he steps out of doors. Urgent speech ends his enquiries for the flowers in 'A Bouquet', left with disreputable neighbours. "What did they make of them? / How long did they live?" He writes strongly and strangely about moorland landscapes, where he trusts his ear, catching, in the stutter of 'Moorside' "the faltering heartbeat of the guns".

Woodward writes extraordinarily well about his children. Unusually, and admirably, his poems become a kind of negative on which the children print their own poem. 'Phoebe' ends with his daughter's triumphant translation of a lamb's cry "I am a baby!" Like Phoebe, he is an excellent mimic, gathering the children's energies, "the little storm of their playing" into his own work.

Strikingly, some of Woodward's more formally disciplined poems seem imaginatively the most open, to space, mystery and new rooms of meaning. In one firmly rhymed piece, a new general lures exhausted troops toward the desert:

> I can promise ten pounds of hay
> For the horses. A gallon of water
> And a bushel of oats a day [...]
> ('Living off the Land')

Woodward's work is most flexible and powerful when it abandons earth altogether, in the long poem 'Ecopoesis', where a planet is "one vast room", and asteroids are "demented / Children [...] in torn frocks of ice". For poetry (like radio) has no limits, and Woodward's poems, escaped from close confinement, create a reality as arresting as Harsent's dark myths, bending the rules which shape Barker's timelines: "The last millionaires fell from the sky / A century ago."

Poetry has many rooms. It can dissolve its reader's preconceptions by passionate intellect, like Barker's quotations, by fire and menace, like Harsent's stories, or, like Woodward's poems, by the commonplace, quietly aslant.

Alison Brackenbury's latest collection, *Bricks and Ballads* was published by Carcanet in 2004. Her new poems can be seen at: www.alisonbrackenbury.co.uk

The Sweet Dance

GEORGE SZIRTES

Matthew Sweeney, *Sanctuary*, Cape, £9, ISBN 0224073451
Sinéad Morrissey, *The State of the Prisons*, Carcanet, £6.95, ISBN 1857547756
James J. McAuley, *New and Selected Poems*, Dedalus, €16, ISBN 1904556355

If one had to draw the co ordinates for Matthew Sweeney they might intersect about the point where Flann O'Brien met Marin Sorescu, though without the latter's more intimate knowledge of bloodliness and tyranny. And there might be the ghost of a flute or pennywhistle there too, because it is impossible to read his poetry without hearing its apparently simple but sophisticated cadences as music.

In fact the music is probably the most important aspect of his poetry. His short anecdotal runs of whimsy-cum-unease are less to do with subject matter or with incident than with pitch. At best they communicate a kind of blessedness like a drunk man dancing along a tightrope.

It is not an easy act to pull off. The balance between whimsy and unease is delicate, and cultivating it does not necessarily make for lightness, or rather it can make for the wrong kind of lightness in which all the clarity, and all the music, remains but somehow the counterbalance of unease is left lying by the roadside and the tightrope walker falls off. There are some poems in Sweeney's new book, *Sanctuary*, that seem thus unburdened and thus a bit lopsided. 'Swim' for instance:

> The skinhead sniggered
> As the duck he had just plucked
> Waddled to the lake.

This is the complete poem. Certainly, it's a haiku and it has some fun with sounds, but it seems rather insubstantial to me, an idea going nowhere significant. And there are others a little like this; longer poems that sway towards us with a certain assurance but then vanish once you get too close.

Then there are poems that dance that old tightrope prettily – but put the foot down a bit hard at the end. One lovely poem, 'UFO', describes a child's experience in Ireland where a UFO lands in the garden. Really it's a poem about the child's relationship with his grandfather and the sense of "alien splendour", where "a copper kettle boiled / away from the fire, / and my grandfather took me / out to the turfhouse / to see the thing being fed..." And all this is rather beautiful and balanced. But the poem's closure ("[...] I closed my eyes, / stuck fingers in my ears / and cried") seems a little too final, a little too self-conscious, especially with the last line all by itself. It is antithetical to Sweeney's own sense of lightness.

Sometimes a poet can take his own gifts a little too much on trust. But there are some very good poems here too, material and manner dancing their sweet dance in properly Sweeneyesque fashion. And top Sweeney is light but haunting.

The power of Sinéad Morrissey's poetry lies in sharply pitched precise emotion and a fine ear and eye for texture. The beauty of her short poems is keening, compact and yet airy. Two poems on facing pages of her new book *The State of the Prisons*, 'Lullaby' and 'Contrail' sum this up. This is 'Lullaby':

> When I can't sleep, you speak to me of trees.
> Of the bald-eyed Eucalyptus
> that flared in your back yard
> like an astounded relative –
> pointing to the honey bees in their rickety hives
> your brother had abandoned.
>
> Sometimes the tree was avuncular.
> Arch with its secrets.
> How it boasted, on days
> your mother
> hung sugarwater,
> the delicate surgery of hummingbirds.

The tone of intimacy is immediately established then shifts twice, through two highly active lines about the Eucalyptus (*bald-eyed, flared*), to a startling simile. Now we are in family-anecdotal land of the kind often found in Sweeney. The second verse continues the family theme, extending the identification of tree with family, but ends in a surprising, wholly discovered image that shifts the poem and launches it off into the unknown, with the lightest of closures so you'd hardly notice anyone had gone out. Despite the active language that constitutes elements of the texture, points at which the mind and eye move fast, there is a surprising spaciousness about the poem that holds its main subject in easy syntactic structures while flittering away like mad in the analogous imagery, seeking something, then finding it.

Morrissey also works on longer set pieces, such as an attractive series of travel pieces about China ("[...] town after coal-dusted town / stream by in the rain"), in which she plays with form as well as with tone, ending on a nice childlike throwing up of hands at the sheer size of the project. Her feeling for

the grip, hammer and drift of language is excellent. ("I want to hap you up //
So that you stagger off [...]") However, I am not sure if her title poem, about
the prison reformer John Howard, is her best work. It seems a little literal to
me, perhaps even a touch over-methodical in its performance: unusual for a
poet of such sharpness and concision. There are poetic effects and good lines
in a narrative that could, I feel, be better told as prose. Morrissey is violin
rather than church organ.

I am sorry not have come across James J. McAuley's poems before. There
would have been time, but he has spent years in America and it turned to
Ireland only in 1998, having been, as Paula Meehan so nicely puts it in her
introduction, "ripped untimely from the bars off Grafton Street". She goes on
to remark that the fifties did not end in Ireland until the end of the seventies.
McAuley was born in 1936 and left Ireland in 1966, when the fifties were still
going strong. His poetry has breathed North American air since then, and
there are elements of late Yeats, Frost and early Lowell in his straight,
handsome, formal verses ("The air of an old song's in my head" begins one
of the best of his mid-seventies poems, 'After the Blizzard').

If Sweeney is pipe and Morrissey violin, then McAuley is a deeper
hunting horn sound. It's a masculine kind of verse: its grandeur is direct, the
emotion clear and deepening, the manner verging on perfectly credible
bardic. He has a very good ear, so he doesn't become trapped in post-Yeatsian
cadences but probes intelligently, lengthening or shortening the line so as to
ease off the grand style. Now and then I think, particularly in poems with a
religious or political theme, he pushes too hard at an open door (the mantra
of our period must be *lightness*), but that's a matter of taste. Few would now
write a line like, "Was it Onan made him vain, pale?". Classical euphemism is
not a natural resource for the times but his poems about family have a grace
and beauty that is noble without any trace of awkward classicising. The
tighter the form the better he often is, such as in 'Rondel':

> After argument the words slow down.
> You, the accused, are revealed as innocent,
> And I, the judge, must toss aside my gown,
> > After argument.
>
> But I'd like to know exactly what you meant
> By that last term of endearment – I must be *shown*.
> *Move* to appeal! Your words misrepresent
>
> The case, whatever you say – and it's well known
> The naked truth will make this judge relent...

> Or at least reduce the sentence to a frown,
>   After argument.

Out of some minor matter comes a beautifully made toy to present to the "you" of the poem. The diction slightly grand, it is, nevertheless, as the baker in Raymond Carver's story says: *a small good thing* A human thing.

George Szirtes was awarded the 2005 T. S. Eliot prize for *Reel*

ℬ

Poetic Geometries

ROBERT POTTS

Rod Mengham and John Kinsella, eds. *Vanishing Point*,
Salt, £14.99, ISBN 1876857137; Mark Strand, *Blizzard of One*, Waywiser Press,
$15, ISBN 0375701370; Yang Lian, *Concentric Circles*, trans. by Brian Holton
and Agnes Hung-Chong Chan, Bloodaxe, £8.95, ISBN 1852247037

In 1963, a young J. H. Prynne, reviewing an anthology of modern German poetry, noted the profound difference between Europe and England when it came to, not only modernism, but the manner in which modernism might be talked about: "the more radical nature of poetic 'modernism' within the continent of Europe, and its close associations with a philosophical climate very different from our own, has produced a peculiarly distinctive mode of criticism and literary discussion". The writer also noted "the gap between the intellectual climates responsible for Larkin or Hughes on one side, and Ingeborg Bachmann or Paul Celan on the other". Forty years on, the point still has some force.

Vanishing Point, edited by Rod Mengham and John Kinsella, is an anthology of "new modernist poems", establishing that in England and English-speaking nations (the US, Australia, and New Zealand, in this case), modernism has continued – "they are not postmodernist, but late modernist writers". Since the definition of both these terms is heavily disputed, and the latter in particular is promiscuously abused, this distinction would have been worth making at greater length.

This is not a themed anthology, nor a canonical one; its selections are suggestive rather than exhaustively representative. Mengham explains the title: "The vanishing point lies beyond the horizon established by the ruling conventions, it is where the imagination takes over from the understanding". It is with regard to "literary conventions" that modernist writing sees a problem which non-modernist work does not. In the latter, a grasp of conventions by poet and reader is the key to successful literary exchange; in the former, both are concerned with exploring the areas of thought and experience which those conventions exclude. There are, necessarily, political implications here, which John Kinsella's rather swift and breathless introduction alludes to; though perhaps a little speedily for any reader not already au fait with the terms he employs.

What is enjoyable about *Vanishing Point*, as an introduction to some of the poets and styles it represents, is its remarkable variety. There are thirty-two writers, including Brian Catling, Roy Fisher, Susan Howe, Lisa Jarnott, Tony Lopez, Barry MacSweeney, Anna Mendelssohn and John Wilkinson. (The editors also include their own work; an approach which I am honour-bound to gently deprecate.) Each, as the introductions suggest, offers an interestingly different approach to the "lyric". There are varying degrees of linguistic and formal self-consciousness, and a frequent, deliberate refusal of certain rhetorical and formal conventions. Decisions of style are, for these poets, intimately connected to political and philosophical commitments.

The best are mobile, various, unsettling; the weaker seem to dully and dutifully reproduce lessons from the library and the seminar (modernism, after all, accrues its own conventions and routines, and its own "vanishing point" is therefore always moving). There are far more of the former than the latter. Indeed, the collection begins with some of John Ashbery's languorous, aleatory lyrics, in which irony and passion weave in and out of each other and to remain still would be fatal: humorous, abundant pieces, spending only seconds on ideas from which other poets might make whole books.

Mark Strand's *A Blizzard of One*, for example, is described as having " a wit reminiscent of John Ashbery", which is a little misleading. Although Strand evidently admires Ashbery, beginning one poem with a line from the latter, he lacks Ashbery's full tonal range. Where, in Ashbery, a note of plangent disappointment, perhaps undercut by a shift into comic bathos or wry amusement, will be only one element in a more various and abundant symphony, in Strand it is virtually the only note.

Again and again, an exhausted elegiac gesture is performed in a knowing and self-mocking tone. The lines "Boredom sets in first, and then despair" and "This melancholy moment will remain" are each used, with predictable aptness, as refrains in villanelles. Across the whole collection, one is left with repeated statements of a denial of expectation (since nothing will turn out as expected, leaving us with regret that things were not otherwise), and also, contrarily, a portentous atmosphere of expectation, to give the poem some fake glamour, a little borrowed energy. Strand's hackneyed symbolism stands in stark contrast to Ashbery's dynamism, intelligence, vitality and colour.

If Ashbery represents one form of Modernist lyric in *Vanishing Point*, then J. H. Prynne can perhaps be taken as another pole altogether. In Prynne's late work, each poem *in its entirety* becomes the context in which any element of it might be understood. (This makes it slightly surprising that *Vanishing Point* publishes only an excerpt from *Red D Gypsum*.) Prynne's poetry works not line by line, but by dispersing and disposing its elements across its stanzas; motifs, syllables, phonemes, allusions and semantic fields relate to each other across the space of the entire poem.

Prynne, as much as any modernist since Pound, has been interested in Chinese poetry; and his own practice is appreciated by many Chinese readers. Yang Lian's *Concentric Circles*, and its excellent essays by the poet and by his translators, give an incidental insight into why this might be; and into how a language determines what "meaning" is available to a speaker unless he or she struggles against it. (Lian, now living in exile, was one of the 'misty' poets, avant-gardists who refused to produce the social realist propaganda prescribed under Mao, and whose work was only briefly tolerated, mainly because the authorities did not understand it.)

As Yang Lian has written elsewhere,

> Strictly speaking, Chinese has no 'grammar' as defined in the West: describing a specific action or thing with meticulously defined person, tense, part of speech and number. One of the salient features of Chinese is that the form of the verb remains unchanged however the person and tense change. Here the Chinese language abandons particularity for abstractness. It implies that 'now' does not exist and there is only language. Once written down, 'this' person, 'this' action and 'this' moment become something universal. Writing is synthesis rather than analysis.

Concentric Circles, in this translation, gives the English reader a valuable (and exciting) sense of the extraordinary difficulties in understanding a completely foreign sensibility and philosophy, and, like *Vanishing Point*, offers a glimpse of the limitations and difficulties of our own.

Robert Potts is an editor at the *Times Literary Supplement*.

Look At These

WAYNE BURROWS

Helen Farish, *Intimates*, Cape, £9.00, ISBN 022407279X
Anna Wigley, *Durer's Hare*, Gomer, £7.99, ISBN 1843234988X
Lucy Newlyn, *Ginnel*, Carcanet, £8.95, ISBN 1903039746
Jane Griffiths, *Icarus On Earth*, Bloodaxe, £7.95, ISBN 1852246952

Helen Farish certainly knows how to get a reader's attention, as 'Look At These', the opening poem in her debut collection testifies with its exuberant equation of breasts and poems. "Suddenly I'm offering them / like a woman ready to mate", she writes, "Don't tell me not to". It's a striking calling card, but Farish is a much more elegiac and nuanced poet than 'Look At These' might initially lead you to expect.

Of three other poems taking breasts as their subject here, only one, 'Biopsy', shares a similar *joie de vivre*, and in that, as the title implies, the speaker's initially celebratory desire to run away "with my breasts / to Barcelona, the Canaries [...] for some seafront life, / fishermen, local wine" is shadowed by cancer:

> I understand the lump now,
> how the cells got together
> in a crescent like a young moon [...]

In 'Surgery', Farish recalls a woman "who chose to have her breasts removed / rather than live with the fear", while in 'Drifts' the weight of her breasts is described painfully shifting, "shaping and reshaping in the night" like a snowy landscape, as she comes to a warm, yet tentative accommodation with her own body.

In these poems the body is an unreliable thing, tied to memory, its mortality apprehended directly through the senses, especially in the poems attempting to come to terms with a father's death. In these, memory is inextricably bound to material things, like the apple orchards of 'July', the "silver Cortina / in the yard" of 'Treasures', or – in a different context – the nine suitcases of the woman in 'Blindfolded', who returns to the occupied Hungary she is fleeing rather than give up seven of them at the border.

In contrast stands the lightness of the drifting whale of 'Mesplodon Pacificus', breaching out of the ocean, creating "an opening into which I pour", or the mother observed in 'Grant Us Time To Read And Ponder' "content / to be making mistakes" that buy her time to think in the pantry.

Best of all is the concluding 'Coffin Path Poem', an epigram on the fleeting nature of existence as quietly devastating as Derek Mahon's 'Days':

> My habit of late night walking
> will mirror my life, how in its twilight
> I'll rush out saying, how beautiful –
> has it been like this all day?

Anna Wigley's *The Bird Hospital* marked the emergence of a poet with a sharp eye for natural description, and a way of making poems of landscape and animal life very much her own. Her second collection has moments of similarly singular vision, like 'The Seabed', with its Shakespearean metamorphoses of a lover's body, 'Cathay's Cemetery', with its "stone angels ten feet high" and "trees / singing elegies in the wind", or the 'Winter Beeches' seen through a "smoke-blue January dusk".

Given the way her debut managed to sidestep obvious influences, it's odd that Wigley's second collection feels less certain of its voice than the first. 'The Jackdaw In The Wind' is little more than an accomplished pastiche of 'The Hawk In The Rain', and echoes of Hughes crop up regularly throughout the book, most obviously in the 'Snowdrop' facsimile 'Marigolds' and the 'Full Moon And Little Frieda'-derived 'The Moon At 3am'. This tendency to echo gives *Durer's Hare* a transitional feel, as though its author is belatedly working something through her creative system.

If Wigley's own eye is filtered through other poets' devices too often here for the collection to feel entirely successful, individual poems still shine out. 'November Trees' might close with the cod-Hughesian trees "striding out to meet the northern waters / with no protection, their thighs like iron", but it begins with "The lamps are going out one by one. / The wind is breathing on them", which is very much Wigley's own coinage.

In 'Shells', 'Sea Lions', 'Crab' and 'Home', a quirkier, more distinctive sensibility remains at work. If this is the transitional book it appears to be, it will be interesting to see where Wigley goes next. In 'The Heart's Crumb', she shows herself to be a lyric poet worth keeping faith in:

> The human heart
> planted in its crumb of soil
> sends out ingenious tendrils,
> wrings oceans
> from a single moisture drop,
> clutches the particle of earth
> till it becomes a field.

Lucy Newlyn's *Ginnel* concerns itself with the mapping of a particular area, in this case Headingley and Meanwood in Leeds. The ginnels of the title are passageways between houses, and the collection uses these as the connecting threads of a local geography, as well as, metaphorically, the implicit link between Newlyn's detailed recall of a 1960s childhood and her present self, who adds the book's nostalgic tone from thirty years' distance.

The world evoked is one of vanished tanneries, pig farms, rag and bone men; of blackberrying, tadpole catching and 'Bryan's Fish Shop', where "cod are left in a hot sea, sizzling" then "hauled in crispy golden and wet / from the scalding spit and spatter of fat" to be "wrapped in a wad of *Yorkshire Post*". In 'Juan Taught Me', Newlyn lists a set of childhood accomplishments and discoveries, from "how to knot a conker string, / when I should mind my own business, / why nettles don't always sting", to "why it was odd / not to... go to church, or believe in God", ending with a wish to be "a boy and working class".

In 'Walls' she affectionately recalls "the curt sound of the vowels" of local speech, "the consonants sturdy as footings / or knobbly as topstones", and 'Bandstand' takes in "a Lowry picture" from a springtime woodland, "daffodils stirring / like a bright fringe under a dark coat", while music drifts "lightly, debonairly, down".

Although vivid and well drawn, the parade of memories lacks a strong purpose. Newlyn rarely acknowledges a larger social world, preferring the personal, elegiac tone, and her poems are strangely depopulated, their people seen in undifferentiated groups, at a distance, as elements in the picturesque scenes. This makes it hard to feel very involved or moved, and the book is rather less than the sum of its parts. It's enjoyable, and finely crafted, but also, finally, as superficial as one of those collections of sepia toned "bygone" photographs so beloved of local newspapers.

If ever a book needed a sympathetic, rigorous editor, Jane Griffiths' *Icarus On Earth* is it. Even after several attempts to unravel them, the poems seemed to slide off the mind, leaving little, if anything, behind. Partly it's the awkward rhythms, the apparently arbitrary switches between flaccid, long sentences, endlessly elaborating on hazily focused images, and sudden, abrupt halts, as seen in 'Floating Poem':

> I give you the summer – evenings, salt on the lip
> of two blue-green glasses, and heat viscous
> as the citrus twist in a highball. Like abroad,
> echoes up the marble stairwell to your flat,
> the spyhole, the static on the entry-phone,
> the smell of cat. The carrying back a whole

net of lemons. Like abroad, too, sleeping beside
ourselves in the long light hours while outside
someone called the shots in that everlasting
game of tennis, and the cats drifted in and out
of our consciousness, saw fair play from tiers
of flowerpots on the balcony, or skittered
the corridor like a shot of ice that twists from
the fingers and containing glass, through open
doors and out, into the Bombay sapphire sky.

It's far from clear that the random lineation, nebulous, meandering effect
and bafflingly clumsy syntax in the penultimate line are intentional, or
deployed to any particular purpose. Griffiths might occasionally read like an
aspiring John Ashbery, but there's little evidence of the humour or surreal
twisting of expectation that makes his work, when it is, so compellingly
(rather than merely) abstruse, and nowhere is this lack of focus more
damagingly seen than in the title sequence.

'Icarus On Earth' relocates the famous myth to contemporary English
suburbia, reworks it from the multiple viewpoints of a mother, a girl next
door, a biographer and Icarus himself, among others, and takes thirteen
pages to say a great deal less than Auden managed in the final eight lines of
'Musée des Beaux Arts'. There's the occasional poem, like 'Valediction' or
'Elayne' that rises above the general morass, but too few to counter the sense
that this is essentially a set of early drafts, often promising, but in serious
need of further work.

Wayne Burrows's collection *Marginalia* appeared from Peterloo in 2001.

℘

Footfalls in the Woods

LESLEY BANKES-HUGHES

Alice Oswald, Woods etc., Faber, £12.99 ISBN 0571218520

Many reviewers of Alice Oswald's work have, quite rightly, chosen to source her poetical heritage; her poetry is imbued with the echoes and 'footfalls' of Eliot, Hughes, Dylan Thomas, Heaney, Hill (and let's not forget Marvell, Clare, Hopkins, and, I would venture to add, W. S. Graham). Such comparisons are inescapable; Oswald is so obviously at home in the tradition of poets who seek to tease out and capture the *genius loci*. The wonderful clarity and exuberance of her descriptions, her tussle with the sinew and gristle of language and her attempts to articulate all the dimensions of what is seen (and unseen) in the natural world, all mark her out as an extraordinary nature poet who controls the (often mercurial) scope and depth of her subject matter with a confident mastery of form and rhyme. All these qualities are certainly to be found in *Woods etc.*, but there is a new underlying tension in the book; a suggestion that the 'nature poet' label may be becoming less satisfactory, more restrictive for Oswald.

If Oswald has absorbed all these earlier poetic influences in her work, it is this finely-tuned receptivity which is the hallmark of her relationship with, and descriptions of, nature. Many poems in *Woods etc.* strive for a perception of the simultaneous forces and counter forces within nature. There are life cycles, metamorphoses, harmonies, antagonisms, all drawn through Oswald's familiar images (real and symbolic): water, bone, woods, stone, moonlight. As in *Dart*, there is the preoccupation with how to reconcile the disparate aspects of nature, how to get a grip on the 'slip-shape' of things, and how, ultimately, to glimpse the spiritual force behind all this apparent randomness. In 'Birdsong for Two Voices', the notational harmony achieves a calm "steady state":

> it gathers the yard with its echoes and scaffolding sounds,
> it gathers the swerving away of the sound of the road,
> it gathers the river shivering in a wet field,
> it gathers the three small bones in the dark of the eardrum;

All this searching around in the natural flux for, to borrow from Hopkins, the 'thisness' (*haecceitas*) of things can be dizzying stuff. In this collection, the importance of *etc.* in the title cannot be overstated: you get the impression that Oswald might spend some considerable time pondering the specks of dust in a shaft of light before looking at what was actually being illuminated.

Dart closed with the Protean river merging into the sea, and 'Sea Poem', which opens *Woods etc.*, takes up this theme of change: "oscillation endlessly shaken / into an endlessly new structure." What made *Dart* so successful, apart from descriptions as thrilling and daring as a first reading of Hopkins, was the way the chorus of voices shaped and paced the work. The different voices gave the river its momentum just as much as its geographical course, and the river, as place and symbol, also held together the poem's layers, threads and ambitiousness.

Clearly *Woods etc.* doesn't, and couldn't, repeat this format. The collection hangs together through shared themes and ideas, but it can sometimes feel as though each poem is unrelentingly searching for the same spiritual 'knowingness', some sort of 'epiphany', however fleeting:

> right here in my reach, time is as thick as stone,
> and as thin as a flying strand
> ('Marginalia at the Edge of the Evening')

As the crickets sing in 'Five Fables of a Length of Flesh':

> [...] we are seeking
> to be slightly more precise than is possible,
> whizzing around, trying to unconceal things,
> literally momentary.

And the emphasis on the natural cycle in all its guises, whether leaf, seed or river, can make for a sense of 'here we go again' in some of these poems. An element of discursiveness sometimes creeps in, bringing with it a slight suggestion of De Quincey's prose (although by no means as unstoppable).

Curiously, in her unquenchable hunt for revelations what marks Oswald out from the poetic crowd is that she doesn't always feel the need for a pat resolution. Her best poems are those which have an open-endedness, or a questioning, such as 'Owl', 'Another Westminster Bridge' or 'Hymn to Iris'. When she attempts to neaten the endings, as in 'The Sea', or 'Marginalia at the Edge of the Evening', her poetry can falter and run out of steam. Oswald is, as always, confident in melding myth and poetic intention. She is sure-footed in her use of traditional form, be it ballad, psalm or, most beautifully, the sonnet; and her deftness and delicacy in using half rhymes is as strong as ever. Her relationship with nature, however, has undergone a subtle change: the natural world is a more abstract, bleaker place to be, and she seems more aware of its darknesses and ambiguities. Man has become more of a cipher, a Bunyanesque figure caught up in the daily repetition of things, unable to make sense of the world, witness Sisyphus, the Danaides, the "fat girl" in the Shamrock Café, or the old couple who "let their hearts sink to one side / and stood in their old clothes, growing frost at the edges."

In the rich accretions of *Dart*, speech was the very texture of the poem. In *Woods etc*, the search for nature's self is expressed as a struggle for articulation, and this sense of the unreleased voice results in a plainer, more pared down and dislocated language: more bone and stone than the eels of the *Dart* ("bright whips of flow / like stopped waves"). Even the presence of the poet has been whittled away, and seems to lodge somewhere in the spaces between the lines as a "wind-born eye", or "the provisional, the inexplicable I".

Alice Oswald is an exceptional poet, and her gifts do shine in *Woods etc*. However, in this collection she seems to find herself somewhere between a rock and a hard place. The book concludes with the spacecraft Voyager 1 floating in space. I'm not convinced that a move away from landscape (real or half-real) and the occasional snapshot of domesticity, into the "Deep Silence" of the ether, is necessarily the most creative direction for her to take.

Lesley Bankes-Hughes is Tower Poetry Administrator at Christ Church, Oxford.

☙

Two Kinds of Utopias

SIMON SMITH

John Kinsella, *The New Arcadia*, W.W. Norton, $27.95, 0393060535
David Herd, *Mandelson! Mandelson! A Memoir*, Carcanet, £7.95,
1857548183

John Kinsella's poetic output is as prolific as his energy for editing and publishing the leviathan Salt with Chris and Jen Emery. *The New Arcadia* continues this forward momentum, taking up the challenge to produce a kind of reply to Sir Philip Sidney's 'The Old Arcadia' and the English pastoral tradition. Formally the book is loosely based on the structure of Sidney's long poem. More important, the core of Sidney's ideas for his revolutionary work, revealed in a correspondence with Languet from 1574, are also the foundations, in Kinsella's book, of the Aristotelian fundamentals "of moral philosophy which treats of justice and injustice". Kinsella's contemporary bearings are rooted in an ethical landscape reminiscent of the early Prynne of *White Stones* or *Kitchen Poems*. Kinsella's book is driven by equal moral fury and sense of injustice, this time at the destruction of the environment, the poverty and cruelty of 'red-neck' culture, the appalling treatment of Australia's Indigenous peoples, and the mass industrialization of the Australian rural landscape shredded through the matrix of global capital.

The book is organized into five sections or 'Acts', loosely along the lines of Sidney's classic, and it is the eclogues, and the series of 'Reflectors' that head up each section, which give the book its shape. For me these discursive poems are the strongest and give backbone to the volume, culminating in 'Reflectors: Drive 5' and its hiatus of unremitting progress as the speaker's car crashes through the landscape causing the annihilation of native fauna:

> I break, I swerve, I accelerate into the curve [...]

> insects caught on the mesh of the grille,
> enfolded in the radiator [...]
> the pump working hard as a heart.
> The pump as a heart? Vice versa?
> Thermostat regulating flow?
> Radiator: heat exchange, fins and tubes,
> inlet and outlet, air flow, turbulator,
> gnats, mosquitoes, flies, and dozens, possibly
> hundreds of species genetically compacted [...]

This is a bleak outlook, in all senses with nowhere left to run, or in the case of this book, nowhere left to drive, for this is a road movie of a book. It is like Kerouac's endless roll of paper winding up the typewriter and across the tarmac, rushing towards Infinity, the West Coast or the end of time. The impending sense of chaos, of a world laid waste and heading, relentlessly, towards its end, makes for an atmosphere of claustrophobia, curious in describing a landscape of expanse. I am left with the queasiness of that first scene in *Mad Max 2*, where the camera is slung underneath the front fender of Mel Gibson's car, leaving the viewer jolted back in his seat fearful of being smashed into the road surface, force-fed the highway itself. The tarmac is the place from where this speaker makes most of his observations – there is the sense of being chauffeured from one (nightmarish) 'bucolic' scene to another in the inescapable whiff of gasoline streaming on the breeze. Strikingly, the book reveals a myth of endless journeying through a kind of Utopian super-realism, a chemical vision of rural Western Australia in eye-watering Technicolor, detailed through the flora and fauna mostly torn to pieces by men in the names of survival, husbandry, or outright sadism.

David Herd's *Mandelson! Mandelson! A Memoir* presents quite different forms of utopianism and myth-making. A reader who expects to find insider knowledge or a potted verse biography of Peter Mandelson will be sorely disappointed. The book asks what it means to know a person only through their image, or a stream of images morphing through time and the media, which only stop at the sound-bite. The answer is – peripherally; and might account for the seeming irrelevance of our politics and the mounting apathy that greets it. This book is a side-long glance at Mandelson the myth-maker, the conjuror of New Labour, the man who transformed the image of the Labour Party into the red rose, a stuttering, Steinian rose. 'A Note on the Title' at the close of the book fills in the detail, addressing readers of the distant future when Peter Mandelson might well be forgotten:

> Peter Mandelson was a politician. An aesthete by temperament, and sometime Director of Communications, his most enduring contribution was symbolic, changing the emblem of his party from a flag to a rose; a rose; a rose; a rose.

Paradoxically, Mandelson is more present through his absence, in a sort of spin on the king of spin. There is a sense of him being there behind the scenes of these poems, but often literally only in name; in the name of 'Peter's Poem' or the silences of 'Peter! Peter! a Noh Play'. The media is the substance, the image (symbol) more real than the individual; the photograph more real than the man. Mandelson exists at the symbolic level only, in a short-hand for Being – in the flickering blue TV strobes he's a talisman, under the cold scrutiny of a photograph the darker edge to our collective happiness.

The book examines ways to live in the shadow of this myth-making and the re-telling of our history and near present through the fish-eye of media and spin. It sets about asking the same questions millions of us were asking in those long-distant days of May 1997: "The question is, 'Are you happy?'" so the 'Disclaimer' teases in the book's first pages. The poems answer the question with aesthetic solutions deceptively flip and light; Herd has obviously learnt a good deal about making serious points with a lightness of touch from the New York School, especially Ashbery and O'Hara. But second and third readings do uncover serious political questioning and, towards the end of 'Disclaimer', a utopianism with echoes of Lloyd George's "fit country for heroes to live in", is revealed alongside the ghost of a socialist Promised Land we can associate with Mandelson's grandfather, Herbert Morrison, and the Atlee government. This is the utopia we are still waiting for, after the broken promises to ordinary people of a hundred years:

> I nodded to a neighbour, who sort of nodded back, made my way to the high street, because all that persists does in fact alter, past the florist and the bank towards the new building. [...] There are to be a number of houses above a row of shops, a hall where on Mondays and Thursdays people will be able to learn Pilates, Tuesdays cookery, Fridays Ceroc; changing facilities; a meeting house; a forum for debate; a well resourced public library, featuring, in particular, extensive holdings in Greek and Roman thought – a first edition of Rabelais. [Whatever.]

The rest of the book is a *tour de force* display of wit and technique, terrific poem after terrific poem. 'Modern Love' beautifully, lyrically unfolds the day-to-day movements of a domestic life against the background of Peter Mandelson's resignation, mapping the disconnections of a life (happily) lived to the event, momentous for government, the politics and the media:

> There are days,
> Months even,
> When you have to stop –
> Forgetting everything
> That doesn't
> Help...
>
> Sitting, with the themes
> Of your conversation:
> 'Not alone in the world,
> But might as well be.'
> You stand up.
> We stand up.
>
> Not alone but might as well be.

The speaker is curious to find the relevance of this resignation to his life: it is an event that should have some engagement with his daily existence. Exact observations on drinking coffee and the play of tree branches at the window are more urgent and pressing than the latest twist to a political career, however intimately the speaker appears to know "Peter" through the papers, radio and the dead eye of the TV. But this is where we all are, finding connections, relevance and correspondence lacking; subjects trapped within the impossible political questions of our time, between standing up and being counted (a stakeholder), or the eighties Thatcherite mantra that there is *no such thing as society*.

Perhaps one outcome of the London bombings of July 2005, and whatever comes next, will be to prompt answers to these questions with a greater sense of urgency. Rather than the betrayals of spin, smoke and mirrors, false promises and their associated false dawns, both collections observe, reveal and process the deficiencies of these politics. They make the connections: cause answered by effect, substance to counter image-making, meaning to mean more than flat or empty symbols. Perhaps the source of our new politics lies in a new poetics. Are you happy?

Simon Smith is Librarian of the Poetry Library. His two books of poetry are *Fifteen Exits* and *Reverdy Road*.

℘

Surviving Fame and Fortune

THOMAS ORSZÁG-LAND

Willard Spiegelman, ed., *Love, Amy: The Selected Letters of Amy Clampitt*,
Columbia University Press, $41:50, ISBN 0231132867
Saskia Hamilton, ed., *The Letters of Robert Lowell*,
Faber, £30, ISBN 0571202047

Whatever would accomplished poets expect to get out of reading the private correspondence of other accomplished poets, whose best writing is usually available in published print? Gossip, certainly. Willard Spiegelman, editor of *Love, Amy*, says we can also learn about the business of literary activity. Saskia Hamilton, editor of *The Letters of Robert Lowell*, offers us "the private thoughts and passions of a figure unrivalled for his influence on American literature". I read such books for advice on how to survive fame and fortune, if they should come; and how not to.

Spiegelman teaches at Southern Methodist University, Hamilton at Barnard College in New York City. Both their books are intelligently introduced and contain a great deal of sensitively selected, hitherto unpublished material. The lives of both their subjects were marked by some of the same pressures which have shaped ours: the indescribable dreadfulness of the Second World War, to which both responded by intense political activity directed at ending the Vietnam tragedy.

Fame and attendant public pressure came early to Lowell, the rebellious offspring of a New England military family; feeding his intensifying bouts of a manic depression that hurt many people, including himself. He committed a lot of literary and personal trivia to hastily jotted and unrevised correspondence, often reminiscent of the email communications of today, mostly with older writers whom he treated as father figures. These letters portray a giant waltzing on flat feet. Clampitt, the academic daughter of a Midwestern farming family, lived in relative obscurity until her sixties, when her first volume of poetry brought her instant recognition. She judged her own writing by the standards set by such posthumous successes as Dickinson, Hopkins and Keats, and her carefully composed private letters still belong to the art of correspondence as practised in the 19th century.

However, she wrote few literary letters because she was busy writing literature. She knew from the start that "a writer is what I was meant to be". But she never became part of the community of famous poets because, in her own words, "writers are all... conscious of being lonely people" and "the more literary they are, the more miserable they seem as human beings". She had nothing to gain by name-dropping. She does not even bother to say whether she knew Leonard Bernstein, a fellow resident of West 12th Street in New York during the 1940s.

Still, from time to time, she allowed herself to be swept off her feet by the poetry establishment, especially in England. In 1985, she described being:

> entertained by my Faber editor, Craig Raine, and his wife Lee, who is a grandniece of Boris Pasternak[...] We were taken to Garsington, a country house where the Bloomsbury crowd used to gather, now owned by an OPEC millionaire, and sat in the hammock in the garden contemplating the pool where the likes of D. H. Lawrence and Aldous Huxley once strolled [...].

But her correspondence with Raine and other editors shows that she knew her own mind, while remaining open to advice. She was annoyed by feminist critics who attacked her for an intellectual approach and temperament, a commitment to so-called high culture and the exuberantly descriptive style of her nature poems. They might instead have respected her for her passionate political activism and public disapproval of the institution of marriage, which she held almost to the end. Unlike Lowell, she thought of discretion in correspondence as a virtue. She liked men, but the identity of her lovers is almost never revealed in her writing. Her last great love was Harold Korn, a professor of law, whom she married only months before her death. In their happiest times in Maine, the two followed a strenuous routine also described by Virginia Woolf writing of her life with Leonard: writing in the morning, walks in the afternoon, reading in the evening.

Clampitt had a huge stamina for public affairs, in the realms of race relations, social welfare and the peace movement, which occasionally resulted in her arrest. Her formal political protest letters addressed to high officials, such as Henry Kissinger while he served as Secretary of State in the Nixon White House, display devastating clarity: one such letter in the 1970s analyses Kissinger's own writing on Indochina and assesses with icy logic the inconsistencies between his own conclusions and policies. It would be good to be able to believe that this letter had contributed to the end of the war.

Just as I am very pleased that at least some of Lowell's letters have proved ineffective. In 1943, when I was dodging the gas chambers of eastern Europe, Lowell wrote to President Franklin D. Roosevelt to announce his refusal to fight Nazism because he feared, quite wrongly, that the Allied policy of seeking unconditional surrender would result in the permanent destruction of Germany as well as Japan. More than two decades later, when he could no longer plead youth or ignorance, he still defended that position in a letter addressed to the Editors of *Partisan Review*. In 1956, when I was under Soviet fire in Budapest in defence of democratic values, egged on by the *Voice of America* promising American assistance that was never sent, the voice of Robert Lowell might just have made a difference. And this is what he did say, in a letter to William Meredith:

> The Hungarians! They are a nightmare of guilt to me [...] I have a Hungarian-American girl in my class who writes me bad love poems. I have ordered her to buy and memorize Marianne Moore and keep for a Christmas present.

At his death in 1977, Lowell was treated by his obituarists as one of the greatest poets of his time, on a level with Auden, Eliot and Yeats. By the time he reached his 30s, he had been on intimate terms, as far as correspondence allows, with the most accomplished poets writing in English (Clampitt, of course, excluded). This made for an enormous volume of correspondence of which only a fraction has found its way into Hamilton's book. His letters, full of literary gossip, fulfil a need to prolong relationships between lonely souls committed by their craft to lives spent in lonely rooms staring at sheets of paper. He complains to his friend and mentor Ezra Pound that Ford Madox

Ford, who employed Lowell as a secretary in 1937,

> would hardly speak to me half the time because (God Damn
> it!) he thought I would write undignified gossip about him in
> old age and, on the strength of that I suppose, become
> president of Harvard.

He could be very unkind and sometimes even silly. This is how he describes to Elizabeth Hardwick a feminist academic exploiting the suicide of Sylvia Plath, who had been his student:

> There was a similar ghastly Plath meeting here last spring,
> with Greer who would read poetry to illustrate her points. I've
> hardly met the real Lesbian storm troops, but I think they talk
> like hysterical Negroes and other fanatics – the meaning of
> words, the objects they denote, mean nothing.

Some of these letters were written during bouts of manic depression when he might say or write things that he would deeply regret later. Yet those who loved him remember an affectionate, courtly, attentive and gregarious poet. Perhaps even literary letters only ever tell part of the story.

Thomas Ország-Land is a poet and foreign correspondent who writes for the *Guardian / Observer* news service and *The Times Literary Supplement*.

℘

Her Dark Materials

JESSICA YORK

Rebecca Horn, *Bodylandscapes*, 26 May–29 Aug 2005,
Hayward Gallery, South Bank, London,
Moon Mirror, St Paul's Cathedral, 27 June–13 July 2005

If you have watched the grand piano, in Tate Modern, judder into life and spew out its innards with a crashing discord, you have come across the work of Rebecca Horn. Her recent show at the Hayward Gallery included some of her earlier body-extension harnesses – one a face-mask stuck with blunt pencils. She can draw with the apparatus but it has no specificity – it's a head-butt of a drawing. Some of her machines are also included in the Hayward show: they teeter and hover and rush into action like inexperienced stilt walkers having trouble with their co-ordination. Horn's choice of materials – feathers, knives, rocks, sheet music – has been a way of introducing evocative references into austerely minimal and beautifully controlled work. In the Hayward exhibition and in her installation at St Paul's she goes further. To introduce elements of metaphor and narrative into the work whilst sustaining her visual style, she takes a lesson from her own feature films, including 'Buster's Bedroom', and includes music specially composed by Hayden Chisholm and her own poetic writing, sometimes as song lyrics and in one piece as the material out of which the work is made.

The integration of her poetry and visual work is most complete in the installation called 'Light Imprisoned in the Belly of the Whale'. Horn has created a contemplative space around a shallow central pool across which move overlapping lines of her poem; projected on to the water and reflected on the walls. Every so often a spindly, mechanical pointer stirs the water, sending ripples through the text till it dissolves:

> In the night words are wandering
> like shadows in the head [...]

The work's title, and lines like "endlessly alone in slippery corridors", attempt to transform the experience of a darkened room into something more elemental and suggestive of Jonah and rebirth. The presence of reflections and ripples, the disappearance and emergence of words and the whale-like music all enhance this suggestiveness.

Maybe words seem like the most readily available way of opening up the narrative and evocative possibilities of an art form that has squeezed story out from between the cracks for almost a century; however, when you step outside and read the whole poem on the wall it's a bit disappointing. The traditions of twentieth century art are very different from those of poetry. Poetic control is embedded in the whole structure of the text. Although the visual artist's control of this whole installation is immaculate, its words are left to resonate with the viewer in an open ended way. They are, after all,, only one of the materials out of which the work is made.

Jessica York is an art historian, film-maker, and poetry café manager.

ॐ

ENDPAPERS

...the need to believe in the Irish language as a vibrant creative power even while it continues to be marginalised in the process of MacDonaldisation...

—Gerard Smyth

Low-down and Reasonably Clean: The Slambasssadors' Review of London Performance Venues

KAYO CHINGONYI AND NATALIE LEER

A team of rising stars of the performance poetry world, the Slambassadors are all past winners of the annual Rise! London Slam *for young people.* Poetry Review *asked them for the low-down on some of the capital's performance venues:*

The Poetry Studio

Natalie: One of my favourite places that I've performed in is the Poetry Studio at the Poetry Society. The studio is an intimate venue, no larger than a living room and kitchen knocked through, so there is no need for automated lighting, firework displays and a sound system to rival Wembley Arena. Instead it is ideal for back to basics poetry as it was meant to be performed. Busts and photographs of established poets decorate the walls, and antique books which have seen these poets, and many more, performing in this space watch reassuringly from their hideaway upon the bookshelf. The key to the studio's charm lies in the intimacy of the space and the simplicity and openness of the lighting, which make it possible to get up-close and personal amid your audience and really communicate with them. To look them in the eye; and for you, and for them, to feel that you are not, in fact, performing, but conversing. No, you're not going to have a gigantic dressing room or laser show, but who needs that, this is poetry.

The Hampstead Theatre: The Michael Frayn Space

Natalie: I like to see my audience. Standing in front of people I can't see, with light blinding me while I fall through a blackness which stares me out, yet gives nothing away, isn't my idea of a fantastic venue to perform in. Fortunately the courteous people at the Hampstead Theatre were offering help with anything I wanted. Lighting, a mic stand, and a cordless microphone were all made available, a well as engineers to both sound-check me and play a CD of music I had composed for backing to one of my poems; and plenty of time was given for a run-through with them. I only used a small section of the stage because it was set up for a play that was running. If you like a considerable stage it would serve well when cleared.

The room sits around 100 people, with the seats getting higher the further back they get, I'm cynical about this type of arrangement because although you're going to get a better view than a flat seating layout, there is rarely enough leg room: so, if like me you suffer knee pain, I advise you sit at the front.

Battersea Arts Centre (the bar/café)

Kayo: Battersea Arts Centre has a number of performance spaces. As part of the "Furnace" creative writing course (run by Apples & Snakes) I was granted free entry into poetry shows held in the bar/café after each fortnightly workshop. This gave me an insight into the dynamics of the venue from a different perspective since I had previously performed in the bar. When performing I found that the location of the stage allows closeness between performer and audience which strips away barriers of formality. The audience were supportive of those reading and clearly very passionate about the spoken word (a capella or with music). As a member of the audience I noticed that the layout and lighting create a wonderful ambience. The stage is located in prime position as a colourful banner draws in the eye. This stage is of ample size for an intimate peformance and could potentially hold a band. On the wall behind it there is a window out onto the main road; however background noise does not affect sound levels inside. The space adapts well to different performance styles giving an open feel to shows. The sound technician was receptive and willing to help. I had a great experience performing at this venue and would definitely recommend a visit.

Stratford Circus

Kayo: There are five useable spaces at Stratford Circus; I performed in a ground floor space as part of *Alphabet Soup* (hosted by Charlie Dark). The stage is fairly large but is raised only slightly from floor level; this makes eye contact easy to maintain and encourages communication between performer and audience. The sound system is excellent, allowing for live vocals and instrumentation, tunes dropped by the DJ and raw words served a capella. The room is quite spacious, allowing a fairly numerous but still intimate audience. The lighting draws attention to the performers, creating an intense mood. The stage is big enough for a live band, but with the band's instruments on the stage it was somewhat difficult to move about the whole stage (as I often do). There was still some space and an area directly in front of the stage where more linear movement was possible. The sound technician paid attention to requests and adjusted levels when required without the indignant scowl that I have noticed at some venues. All in all this is an exquisite space for poetry and music.

The Globe Theatre

Kayo: Shrouded in history, the Globe is certainly awe-inspiring. This is a large venue (holding 1,600 people at full capacity) yet standing on the stage it did not feel that the audience were very far away like in some large venues. The sound team were good and adjusted to the vocal percussion element of the Slambassadors' live show well. We were allowed plenty of time to sound-check and the backstage area was very hospitable. If not to perform I would certainly recommend a visit to the Globe to take in the atmosphere.

Natalie: The Globe is a place I'd always wanted to visit, so when I was offered the opportunity to perform there I jumped at the chance. It's a beautiful building with so much history it almost feels like you're walking straight into one of Shakespeare's plays. It has an open roof but if it rains a cover is put over. As helpful as the sound team are, the only potential problem with the Globe are the monitors. They are positioned in such a way that it's virtually impossible to hear yourself, which is fine for a play, but for something which relies on rhythm and musicality, like Polyvocal Poetry, it isn't the easiest place to perform.

Kayo Chingonyi had his first poem published at fifteen. He won the *Respect! London Slam* in 2003; and is in his first year of an English degree at Sheffield. Natalie Leer was a winner in the *Respect! London Slam* in 2004; she is a first year student of Performance Arts at Dartington College of the Arts. For Slambassador and *Rise! Slam* details, contact Joelle Taylor, jtaylor@poetrysociety.org.uk

LETTER FROM DUBLIN

GERARD SMYTH

This year's Dublin Writers Festival opened on June 16th, Joyce's Bloomsday – a day that, for many, marks the apotheosis of achievement in 'modern' Irish literature. If the weather permits – and this year it did – the city takes on a festive atmosphere; and any casual visitor could be forgiven for thinking that we belong to a culture where it is second nature to pay homage to the literary arts.

On this particular June 16 you could not only drop in on any number of 'performances' from the Bloomsday manual but living poets too were in good supply, with – to borrow a phrase from Flann O'Brien – "verse speaking bouts" by Kathleen Jamie, Carol Rumens, Milan Richter, Robert Robertson, Gerald Stern, Roo Borson, and Charles Simic. The latter writers were in Dublin courtesy of Canada's very generous Griffin Poetry Prize which, with quite a fanfare, arrived in town *en bloc* to coincide with the festival. Simic, who received $50,000 for his *Selected Poems* in the Griffin's International category, gave a reading along with Canadian winner Roo Borson and several other poets associated with the prize. It seemed to some observers that in all likelihood more Canadian dollars were spent on the Griffin evening than the entire budget for the four-day Festival.

In an introductory address the provider of this beneficence, Scott Griffin, spoke of how happy he was to have his winners in a city where writing and writers are taken seriously. There is something of a myth around Ireland's receptiveness to poets and poetry. Foreign poets heading in our direction have often indicated their excited anticipation at the prospect visiting a true republic of poetry where the art is cherished and honoured as part of the natural order.

How they arrive at such a notion is beyond those of us less inclined to subscribe to such a view. The poet and editor John F. Deane, in an essay published recently in *The Irish Times* declared: "I have never found poetry so ignored in actuality as I do today". Deane's pessimistic view and trenchant condemnation of the value (or lack of it) placed on poem and poet in our newly prosperous land became a talking point. But only briefly: like most attempts to provoke serious consideration of the true state of poetry, it withered on the vine.

Some time ago, poet and translator Michael Smith raised another contentious issue – that again elicited no great response – in the *Poetry Ireland Newsletter*. "I think we should rid ourselves of the notion that by being Irish we somehow have been especially endowed to write poetry, that we are naturally a poetic people". Smith went on to blame this "pernicious notion" for lack of development of " a critical attitude towards the writing of poetry". The proliferation of writing classes was another of his targets and few could argue with Smith's contention that the teaching of the appreciation of poetry is of "far greater importance to the state of poetry".

Meanwhile, the vibrant state of Irish-language poetry owes much to the energy and talents of a poet whose sudden death in June, aged fifty-five, shocked all those who knew him personally and through his work. Cork-born Michael Davitt, whose early work announced the arrival of a distinctive poetic personality, infused the vernacular with a modernist sensibility. The literary journal *Innti* which he founded in 1970 – and its generation of writers – had a revitalising effect on the language and its poetry in that period. There was, at the time in Irish language poetry, something new and innovative about an imagination that went beyond the confines of Ireland and took account of what was happening elsewhere. His response to the world was conditioned by that era: most of the obituaries and tributes paid to him after his death recall how often he had been described as "the Bob Dylan of the Irish language".

Michael once remarked on the need to believe in the Irish language as a vibrant creative power even while it continues to be marginalised in the process of MacDonaldisation which, he believed, was sweeping through this Island of Saints and Scholars. The same MacDonaldisation may be responsible for the marginalisation of poetry that prompted Deane to write his *cri de coeur*.

Gerard Smyth is a poet, journalist, and Managing Editor of *The Irish Times*. His fifth poetry collection is *A New Tenancy* (Dedalus Press, Dublin 2004).

PR JUKEBOX

Poetry Review Jukebox is a chance to replay high points from the journal's past. Requests, for material from issues published before 1995, are welcomed.

In Spring 1972, Eric Mottram produced a conspicuously cosmopolitan issue of *Poetry Review* (63:1):

Tristan Tzara trans. Lee Harwood
small town in siberia

(Petite ville en Sibérie)
written 1916-18, published: *25 poèmes* (1918)

a blue light that holds us flattened on the ceiling
it's as always my friend like a label of hell's gates stuck on a
        medicine bottle
it's the quiet house my friend shudders
and then the heavy bowed dance
presents old age skipping hour by hour on the clock face
the unsullied necklace of cut loco lamps comes down among
        us now and then
and collapses you call that silence to drink tin roofs herring tin's
        gleam and my seemly heart on some low houses lower higher
        lower on which I want to run and rub my hand against the hard
breadcrumb covered table sleep oh yes if only one could
the train once more the fool spectacle of the dandy's tower I'm
        left on the bench
what does the fool the dandy the newspaper what's going to
        happen matter it's cold I'm waiting speak up
hearts and eyes roll in my mouth
get moving
and little children in the blood
(is it the angel? I'm talking about the one who's approaching)
let's run even faster
always everywhere we'll be left surrounded by darkened windows

This translation by Lee Harwood has had a rich subsequent life. First collected in his *Selected Poems of Tristan Tzara* (Trigram Press, London, 1974), it next appeared in his *Tristan Tzara, Chanson Dada: Selected Poems* (Coach House Press/Underwhich Editions, Toronto, 1987) and is now published – in a third country – in his revised and expanded *Tristan Tzara, Chanson Dada: Selected Poems*, forthcoming from Black Widow Press, Boston, December 2005.

℞

Michel Deguy trans. Anthony Rudolf
The hour-glass

from *Poèmes de la Presqu'ile* (1961) part 3 (*Les Jumeaux*)

If I lose the habit of loving you, we are like two retired people gardening, separated by a son thicker than a dyke.

To learn anew: place your left cheek-bone against my right cheek-bone, and knock gently on your nape to pass your eyelashes over me, the sand of your hair, your breath that tastes like fruit.

Every three minutes turn the hour-glass over.

Anthony Rudolf says: Perhaps this revised version could be seen as a cover recording, but by the same singer! To reprint the translation I did thirty-three years ago followed by a revised version makes me feel vulnerable, even though translation is always provisional. I console myself that the earlier version was accepted by Eric Mottram, a tough editor with a good ear, so it can't have been that bad as a prose poem in English. But I prefer my revision:

The hour-glass

If I lose the habit of loving you, here we are like two retired people working in the garden and separated by a son bulkier than a stone pier.

To learn anew: place your left cheek-bone against my right cheek-bone, and knock gently on your nape to bring me your eyelashes, the sand of your hair, your breath that tastes like fruit.

Every three minutes turn the hour-glass over.

Jerome Rothenburg
Peyote Song (Huichol)

climbed the blue staircase up to the sky
climbed where the roses were opening
       where roses were speaking

heard nothing   nothing to hear
      heard silence

I climbed where the roses were singing
      where the gods were waiting
      blue staircase up in the sky

but heard nothing   nothing to hear
      heard silence   silence

Jerome Rothenburg writes: I was very much involved with *Poetry Review* in the 1970s, part of a close connection with Eric Mottram & others, but have lost touch in later years.

Rothenberg, who in PR 63:1 is also translating Native American oral verse, has published more than seventy books of poetry and anthologies. Among the most recent are *A Book of Witness*, his twelfth collection from *New Directions*, and *Writing Through: Translations & Variations* (Wesleyan University Press).

LETTERS TO THE EDITOR

In the *Times Literary Supplement* recently, Yves Bonnefoy (surely a future Nobel laureate, if there is literary justice in the northern world!) observed that "However remarkable [a] text may be, its poetic quality depends on its author having known how to keep alive in it the light of what is beyond language" – thus providing both an implied definition of poetry and a touchstone by which the art may be judged. The context of Bonnefoy's observation was Christopher Ricks's inaugural lecture as Professor of Poetry at Oxford and what Bonnefoy characterises as "the old problem of the distinction between prose and poetry".

It strikes me that John Burnside's essay ("Travelling Into the Quotidian") in your summer issue is a supreme illustration of the fact that prose can be among the best places in which to find poetry. Burnside's piece is at once a critical essay and a prose poem, a traveller's tale and a poetic narrative, an exposition of a hypothesis that "the lyric opens a door in the everyday" into "the otherworld behind the taken-for-granted" and a lucid embodiment of it. That Burnside's essay – no less than his 'Eleven Gift Songs' earlier in the same issue – proves to be poetry at its most transfixing is an ironic, intriguing and auspicious start to a new phase in *Poetry Review*'s editorial history. "Poetry works where maps are useless", John Burnside contends.

The onward journey promises to be a scenic and eventful one…

DENNIS O'DRISCOLL, CO. KILDARE, IRELAND

※

[…] The Carol Rumens review came to my attention because I think that she is a very fine poet indeed […]. Of course, reviewers cannot comment on every poem and must make their judgements according to their lights, but I was a little surprised to see that Rumens' poem 'Outside Oświęcim' does not get a mention. To my mind, this is one of the outstanding poems of the late twentieth century. Rumens is obviously well acquainted with eastern Europe and she handles the human-historical context of Auschwitz powerfully but sensitively. An interesting point about the poem is that, following its publication in *Direct Dialling* (1985) a further three-line stanza, marked as section 23, was added to the poem in her *Selected Poems* (Chatto & Windus) in 1987. It deserves quoting in full: "I died for nothing, no one. I was eighteen; / knew how to love, forgot; was beautiful, / then not. The train slides on across my shadow."

There's not much one can say, or even want to say, after that.

ALEX SMITH, SAFFRON WALDEN

EDITORIAL

Although Rousseau confessed that "my purpose is to display to my kind a portrait in every way true to nature, and the man I shall portray will be myself", it is Dante who gave us the poet as Everyman. His journeyman footslogger sets the course for this *Underworld* Issue. Millenarian anxiety has arrived in London something over five years late, but this July saw it out in force. The Underground never seemed so oppressively hot, its long descending escalators so eerie. Suddenly Everyman, and -woman, discovered the art of walking.

If *terza rima* is the walking pace of the underworld, it's small wonder we generally find it easier to ride there. As this issue's *Conversation* suggests, contemporary British culture leaves walking largely to philosophers of the visual – Richard Long, Marina Abramovic – or tourists of revelation like John Berger and Iain Sinclair. But walking, Yang Lian points out, is "a core forever deepening", a descent into thought. It's the rhythm of Platonic dialogue, through which differences may arrive at agreement. As such it echoes the practice of translation, present throughout this issue of *Poetry Review*.

If Millenarianism is in large part a fear of the unknown other, translation pays it creative attention. This is a practice which respects otherness, while allowing that it can be known. As the Italian philosopher Gemma Corrradi Fiumara says, listening is the "other side" of language. Translation, like the engaged reading poetry demands of us – of which it's anyway a kind – is a form of listening more widely practised in virtually every other literary culture than the Anglophone. And it may be that the turn outwards, so often advocated in current political and social debate, needs to be conducted even at this, the symbolic level of our culture.

Elsewhere in the magazine, Martha Kapos and Joanne Limburg remind us that personal hells can be internal, and not of our making. It's to be hoped that recording planned cuts to national literary institutions isn't going to become a staple of these editorials. Nevertheless, at the time of going to press, it seems that Survivors' Poetry – which has worked nationally, for over a dozen years, with poets and poetry linked to distress and disadvantage – may face the loss of its core funding: with all that would entail of uncertainty, provisionality and the footslog of the fundraising round. We live in anxious times.

FIONA SAMPSON

CONTRIBUTORS

Tom Boll recently completed a PhD on Octavio Paz and T. S. Eliot. He is Assistant Director of the Poetry Translation Centre at SOAS

Colette Bryce has published two collections with Picador.

John Burnside's *The Good Neighbour* is recently published by Cape. His latest novel is *Living Nowhere* (Cape, 2003).

Simon Carnell and **Erica Segre**'s translations of Sciascia volumes are published by *PN Review* and *Forum Italicum*.

R.D. Coleman is a former Commissioner in the Homeless Services Agency of the City of New York. His latest exhibition of photographs is at the Monian Gallery in Lower East Side.

Sasha Dugdale is consultant and translator for the Royal Court Theatre. Her second collection of poetry, *The Estate,* is published by Carcanet/Oxford Poets in 2007.

Menna Elfyn's latest collection is *Perffaith Nam* (*Perfect Defect*) from Gomer. She was Children's Poet Laureate for Wales in 2002–3.

Ruth Fainlight's latest publications include *Sheba and Solomon*, with Ana Maria Pacheco (Pratt Contemporary Art, 2004) and *Burning Wire* (Bloodaxe, 2002).

John Fuller's latest collection of poems is *Ghosts*, shortlisted for the Whitbread Prize. His new novel, *Flawed Angel*, is published by Chatto and Windus this November.

Iain Galbraith's poems and translations have been published in the *TLS*, *Chicago Review*, *PN Review* etc. He was awarded the 2004 John Dryden Prize for Literary Translation.

Katherine Gallagher is an Australian poet resident in London. Her latest collection is *Tigers on the Silk Road* (Arc 2000).

John Hartley-Williams's latest collection, *Blues* (2004), was shortlisted for the T. S. Eliot prize.

Paul Henry's most recent collection is *The Slipped Leash* (Seren).

W. N. Herbert's *The Big Bumper Book of Troy*, and his co-edited anthology *Strong Words: Modern Poets on Modern Poetry*, both appeared in 2002.

Ellen Hinsey is the author of *The White Fire of Time* (Wesleyan/Bloodaxe) and *Cities of Memory* (Yale University Press). She lives in Paris.

Elin ap Hywel was for many years Fiction Editor at Honno, the Welsh women's press. She shares a RLF Fellowship at UCW Aberystwyth with Menna Elfyn.

Martha Kapos's *My Nights in Cupid's Palace* (Enitharmon, 2003) was a PBS Special Commendation and won the Aldeburgh Prize for best first collection. She is Assistant Poetry Editor of *Poetry London.*

Kapka Kassabova is a poet and fiction-writer from Bulgaria who settled first in New Zealand and now in the UK. *Someone Else's Life* was published by Bloodaxe in 2004.

John Kinsella's *The New Arcadia* is due out with WW Norton in the UK in October; Arc will be publishing his poem *America* shortly, while *Doppler Effect: Collected*

Experimental Poems was published by Salt in 2004. He is a Fellow of Churchill College, Cambridge.

Yang Lian was born in Switzerland and grew up in China. A New Zealand citizen, he has settled in London since 1997. *Where the Sea Stands Still* was a PBS Recommendation in 1999; *Concentric Circles* (Bloodaxe, 2005) is reviewed by Robert Potts on p.97.

Tim Liardet's *To the God of Rain* (2003) was a PBS Recommendation. His fifth collection, *The Blood Choir*, which won an Arts Council of England Award, appears from Seren in 2006.

Joanne Limburg's *Femenismu* (2000) was short-listed for the Forward Prize for Best First Collection.

Sarah Maguire is the Founder Director of the Poetry Translation Centre at SOAS. Her books include three collections of poetry and the anthology *Flora Poetica*.

Valeria Melchioretto's first pamphlet, *Podding Peas,* was published in 2004.

Robert Minhinnick's latest collection is *After the Hurricane* (2002). *The Adulterer's Tongue*, an anthology of Welsh-language poetry, was published in 2003.

Eugenio Montale: this late uncollected poem is taken from the third part of the 'Poesie disperse' appendix to Mondadori's *Complete Poems of Montale.*

Sean O'Brien's *Cousin Coat: Selected Poems* 1976-2001 appeared in 2002. His version of the *Inferno* is to be published in 2006 by Picador. He is Professor of Poetry at Sheffield Hallam University.

Pascale Petit has recently published *The Huntress* (Seren) and a chapbook, *The Wounded Deer* (Poetry Business).

Peter Porter's latest of more than twenty collections is *Afterburner* (Picador, 2004).

Sheenagh Pugh lives in Cardiff. Her latest collection, *The Movement of Bodies* (Seren), is a PBS Recommendation.

Rodney Pybus's last collection was *Flying Blues* (Carcanet); in the pipeline is *Veronica Lake.* He is a former co-editor of *Stand* and lives in Suffolk.

Lawrence Sail's essays, *Cross-currents*, are out from Enitharmon this year.

Elizabeth Smither is a New Zealand poet whose *A Question of Gravity: Selected Poems* was published by Arc in 2004.